RISEN

ALA SPECIAL EDITION

RISEN

why libraries are here to stay

the technology that almost took the
library's power away is now giving it back

anthony hodge
bastiaan f. zwaan

Risen - Why Libraries Are Here To Stay
The technology that almost took the library's power away is now giving it back
By Anthony Hodge and Bastiaan F. Zwaan

ALA Special Edition, January 2007

Book design by Taco Ekkel

ISBN-10: 90-78779-01-2
ISBN-13: 978-90-78779-01-8

Preface

Bastiaan and Anthony met just over two years ago. Bastiaan was at a library vendor conference in Denver, Colorado where he was introduced to Anthony through Mr. Ross McLachlan, the Library Services Administrator from Phoenix Public Library. They were immediately drawn to working together because they knew from the first conversation that they both shared the same passion and ambition: to give the world a better OPAC.

Today, Anthony is Marketing and Communications Manager of Medialab Solutions BV in Amsterdam, the Netherlands. Anthony started out shelving books during his university studies, and went on to become a reference provider. Combining his passion and experience in the library world with an education in politics and public affairs, he has always been a natural writer. Anthony is experienced in the practical aspects of a library's activities, with an emphasis on software and other logistical aspects. He is a dedicated contributor to the debate on information sources and their future in an increasingly technological world.

Bastiaan is co-founder, president and CEO of the Amsterdam operation. Today's Medialab, founded in 2000, focuses its efforts and products on the library industry. Bastiaan comes from outside the library world. He holds a degree in ergonomics and product development from the Technical University of Delft in the Netherlands. Bastiaan has founded and acted as CEO of Dutch IT companies in the realm of software development and document management, working closely together with US-based partner companies. Since Medialab began directing all its attention to the library market, Bastiaan has grown into a true fan of libraries and what they stand for.

Together, each with their own perspectives and experiences, they decided to write this book as a sideline to their work at Medialab Solutions.

Medialab has now been active in the international library world for a full two years. Medialab developed AquaBrowser Library, the library system-independent web interface to liberate the library catalog and to aggregate a wide range of internal digital sources, web pages and external subscripted sources. Most importantly Medialab saw that their search technology could make using the library better, easier and more accessible to its target audience. What they've actually experienced in their own AquaBrowser implementations is a substantial increase in the search of the library's collection. What Medialab also experienced is that AquaBrowser Library facilitated the library professionals to easily aggregate digital sources under one single search interface. That is the 'proof in the pudding'. They did not write this book to promote the sales of the AquaBrowser Library. It is the other way around. This book was written to emphasize those aspects they have observed in the library realm that were basically the same reasons why AquaBrowser Library was created.

A perception that's been made along the way is that there is little real innovation and that the library world is very introverted. There is a lot of grumbling going on and a feeling of being threatened by outside developments. These grumblings are not limited to the library professionals, but come also from the library vendor industry.

Despite this, the chances and opportunities seem clear, both for the library and for the parties in the industry. They have a vision to support the emancipation and growth of the public library world.

> "We believe that libraries behave too much as if the technological developments and advancements outside the library world have already taken away its relevance in society. We have written this book as a contribution to that emancipation and to make the library world aware of the opportunities that lie in waiting. And of course we are biased. We do believe the web is not the threat but the opportunity. We believe that the web identity and accessibility are the key elements of success for libraries with a public function. Technology that almost took away the power of the library is now giving it back. This, in combination with the capacity of the library professionals to take up the challenge and to embrace their role as local guide in the land of information, makes this the time for the library to grasp onto those external advancements and return to the front of information providing. The library with a public, regional responsibility is here to stay. We believe the library is likely to 'rise from the ashes'. This is a book about ambition, hidden opportunity, and the ability to focus and self-analyze."

– Anthony Hodge & Bastiaan Zwaan

Table of Contents

It's very possible that given the outlook of the modern library today it could become completely obsolete by the year 2012. Four key elements to turn the tide are recognized and explained.

No commercial, for-profit institution can replace the public library because it cannot claim the role of trustworthy information guide. The library's collection will reflect its social function, in many cases through further specialization.

The mission of every public library is to make its collection as accessible as possible. The reality is that only a small percentage of every community uses the public library as a primary source of information. Web accessibility and search of the collection must be improved for the library's survival.

The library has been evolving in recent years, and is slowly learning to look past automation and collection management. It is the image of the library that actually needs to be changed, not the library itself. The web offers a tremendous podium to make this change.

Risen - Why Libraries Are Here To Stay

Library software could become web-based just resembling the consumer market. Functionality development and user interface will be focused towards real user needs. With this new software paradigm the library can choose the functionality and services necessary to provide the best services for its patrons. ils vendors are likely to follow.

The library will be recognized as a trustworthy and essential guide in the information landscape that can be relied upon. Before 2012 the library can secure its existing role as an inspiring cultural environment that is recognized by anyone to facilitate life long learning.

RISEN

Introduction

By the year 2012, futurist's predictions were coming true. The third wave, the information age, had taken over all aspects of existence. No other form of power retained any importance, except information, information, and information. What had started as a luxury, an option, had quickly become a question of life or death. In order to be on the life side of the debate, one had to be in touch with all that was "mainstream"; the clothes, music, opinions, and politics. Ideology had not died, but become singular: be average or vanish.

The only real struggle that remained in a world of blissful mediocrity was the question as to who controlled the definition of average. Someone or something had to seize the reins of the whole world and channel the information to everyone, so as to prepare the road for an evened out population. And what else, or whom else, if not the Internet and its all-too-powerful search engines would be there for the job. These are mechanisms that create the illusion of free will, but actually distribute the information according to algorithms that are not always as democratic as believed to be.

There was a reality we all had to face. Information, as free and obtainable as it may have seemed, was actually being controlled by an elite few. The Internet grew increasingly larger and evermore expansive, but the actual number of sources of information dwindled to a measly few.

These sources were becoming more controlling, encompassing and ever wealthier.

Information became an increasingly valuable commodity. Those who would control it would do so with the intent to make more money as their number one priority. The technology that society believed was making life easier and making the world smaller, more understanding of our differences, and 'leveling the socio-economic playing field', would ultimately lead to our destruction.

The public library, which had always been a cornerstone in society as the guardian of information, was fading away into oblivion. Corporations were now battling for control, and for the top (and only) position. It would be the most brilliant and legal monopoly the world would ever see.

The public library, or any form of library that is serving a public, broad community (in this context we even tend to include large, broad university libraries too), would become too expensive and cumbersome for society to foot the bill for anymore. And why would communities spend tax money on the library when the services of such enormous companies were so much more advanced and wealthier in resources and funds? What started in 2005 in California (mind you, the 5th largest economy in the world) with small community libraries facing shut-downs, threatened to spread across the world. Larger cities began to look at just how much they were allocating to their libraries in comparison to how many people were actually using the libraries and their services.

> The public library, which had always been a cornerstone in society as the guardian of information, was fading away into oblivion.

Corporations were ready to conquer the world with other money-making solutions and control over digital content. It was all of average quality, but that did not seem to bother any of us actually. The corpora-

Introduction

tions started to flood the Internet with inexpensive, quick and totally average resources and information. Ease of access, the kind that is effortless to digest for the average, non-questioning consumer, was the product. Corporations systematically took over as the only outlets of information, using the Internet as their platform, since it was so easy to take control over it. If there was ever any friction, it was the competition between the now two or three corporations left in the game. As long as their competitive façade remained unscathed, society didn't much question the scenario. After all, as long as it wasn't one single corporation in control, there would never be fear of the totalitarian entity portrayed in Orwellian fantasies.

We, the consumers, forgot along the way that the most valuable information is often hidden in books, journals, articles and archives – all things found inside the library. But starting in 2005: quantity won out, not quality. Saving time and employing the least amount of effort to do something is what the world became all about. In essence it was almost a step back in human evolution. It was like the de-evolving of intelligence. It was all avoidable too.

First, we stopped asking the right questions. Then we stopped questioning altogether.

This all started because we were so naive in our search for valid information. We didn't always know exactly what the best path of questioning or searching was, where the best sources were located. And at some point, we didn't care anymore. When we performed an Internet search, we almost always received a list of answers to any question. We assumed truth in the Internet because we found it on a corporation's search engine and it was, after all, useful. We would take the first, second or third item in the search result list because our lives were too busy and time was too valuable to continue any further. Even worse, our trust in the typical Internet search tool grew. We would just assume that the first set of items at the top of the result set represented the best information available.

Once we stopped questioning everything we were doomed to become average. It was much more efficient for the corporations to offer the 'most commonly' requested information, and simply do away with the rest. It all went so quickly. We chose not to question clothing styles, politics, opinions or anything else. We knew where to find any information to feed our needs. We knew how to discuss and to communicate and exchange experiences, because we knew that information could be collected instantly.

> We didn't see ourselves as average because we had no reason to question anything.

Today in 2006, if society recognizes the story above as a possibility of what 2012 could look like, then it can also see that things luckily haven't yet reached that point. There is an existing and rather significant tool we have to conquer the 'acceptance of the average'. It is the Public Library. The public library is already the guardian of information, the realm and protectorate of the information democracy. It is powered by dedicated people committed to serving the public good, filled with validated facts, opinions, a multitude of qualified resources, a wide array of potential useful technologies and the flexibility and intelligence to cope with our need to have information instantly and conveniently.

In fact, there are only a few things needed in order to avoid the dim and mediocre possibility of accepting the average. In the following chapters we will discuss what we feel are the opportunities for the library itself as well as the library vendor industry, to prove and promote the library as the epicenter and sole institution qualified to provide and safeguard our information:

1. Information Democracy

The library is the public institution representing quality, reliable information. The library has the opportunity to take various sources, in a mix of national and regional perspectives, and aggregate them for the patron via modern web technology. This is because the library's role in society is to function as the central public provider of regional or specialized quality information. The library is responsible for this role: the information guide. It is there to lead information seekers through the landscape of relevant formats, resources and knowledge available to them. It could be recognized as the single institution to do this, because no commercial institution will ever be able to claim this role due to ambiguous objectives and desires (read: profit) that will always stand before the content.

The library represents the information particular to a given region, city, or neighborhood. Every place on the planet has its own story and sub-culture. The library is the first-hand collector of any location's story. This is almost a natural relationship that dates back to ancient society; the library was always given the "expert caretaker" role. The information could be completely general or completely specific to that region, but the important thing to consider is that every library carries the potential power of perspective.

Only a local library can offer a patron the most unobstructed view into a society because the collection of the library will directly reflect the culture, taste, needs and desires of that society. Another way to look at this statement is that an Internet search engine that uses its search to pull information from anywhere and rank it on relevancy built from algorithms will do an amazing job providing general information, but cannot give you the hands-on perspective and personalization of a specific community, region or culture.

Freedom and availability of information is necessary for democracy to prevail within the library. The democratic freedom of choice means that not only does the possibility of freely searching sources exist, but that one should be able to compare the quality of those sources.

If there is any fear that information democracy would make the worlds' libraries too similar, remember that every library caters to its own community. That's who it serves, who it adapts to, and who shapes it. With that in mind, note that no two communities in the world are exactly alike. That means every local library, big or small has something special to offer, something unique to specialize in. If a public library can focus on this kind of home-grown specialization and catering to its community, continue to offer general world information, while blending it all together with the broader collection of literature and non-fiction, then it is moving in the right direction.

2. Search and Accessibility

Most public libraries have public access to their collections stated as the highest priority in their mission statements. The collections, both physical and digital, are maintained and offered with the highest care. However, despite these facts, actual usage of these knowledge sources (both physical and digital sources) is a mere fraction of the usage of the Internet for finding information. If the public library wants to continue to play a vital role in information facilitation, then it would appear that the most obvious way to achieve an increase in usage of the collection comes by giving better access to it through the Internet. There needs to be a revolutionary movement away from what has been such a focus for so many years: collection development.

It is often even smaller changes in the accessibility and layout of library websites that have the biggest positive effect for the users.

Visions, technologies and products that make the search process more attractive, aggregate sources and offer it all in one single interface are already available today. But they are only just being discovered and recognized as reachable means and methods for the library to regain its role as the central, public, trustworthy institution to give access to a carefully selected, aggregated set of quality information.

3. Identity versus Reality

The public library has been evolving in recent years, and is learning to look past automation and collection management. It is the image of the library that is actually so far behind. There is a kind of flexibility that libraries need to uphold in order to keep their patrons returning. And since the patrons are often the financiers of the library, the library focuses all it can to give the patrons what they demand. Libraries are actually in the consumer information and knowledge business. The use of technology to 'compete' with broad Internet searches reaches far and wide in this realm. The content in the library ought to be just as easily accessible as the content found performing a broad Internet search. This brings us back to the concept that the best information can only be found through a multitude of means and sources. It then becomes the library's added responsibility to create and offer a Web environment that can do this all at once, in the best manner possible, in order to remain relevant and efficient to the user.

> Libraries are actually in the consumer information and knowledge business.

Today's society has become obsessed with service. Service in restaurants, airplanes, academic settings, businesses, and non-profit organizations alike are providing services. Service industries account for an ever-increasing percentage of the global economy, from restaurants and airlines to academic institutions and non-profit organizations. It is the quality of the service that people create their impressions of every business. As such, it is the quality of the received services which functions as the basis of consumers impressions of a given organization. It is also the accessibility of the library's services that accounts for this. Accessibility of these services is crucial to an organization's success and even more so where libraries are concerned.

The Internet provides the most efficient way to access library collections remotely. However, not only is it necessary to be able to remotely access the library, but clear and open accessibility to the entire collection can easily be achieved. There are perfect examples of this, such as Queens Library in New York, Amsterdam Public Library in the Netherlands, and King County Library System in Washington state; where not only is the library catalog remotely accessible, but so are the entire digital collections to which these libraries subscribe.

Remote and internal access can, of course, still go wrong. There are plenty of library homepages that are overcrowded with too much irrelevant information and where a direct link to the catalog search is so hidden that the communities served by these libraries would never think to use their library's website as a source of information. This leads people back to the 'reliable' source of search engines which are easy to reach and always provide some kind of instant results.

In order to get people back into their planes, The Dutch airline, KLM, needed focus on service, core assets and reinvent their image via the Internet. There was no real change to the company itself. The accessibility via the Internet appeared to be a key service element, recognized by anyone. KLM with its partner, Air France and its alliance with Northwest Airlines, became one of today's most profitable and highest service-ranking airline that exists today. In order to get patrons back into the library, the library will need to do the same. The key for the library is to reinvent its web accessibility and its web identity.

4. Library Vendor Challenges

The major software players in the ILS (Integrated Library Systems) vendor market are older, established companies. Most parties tend to pay more attention to what their competition is doing than looking after their own users' needs. They keep each others products checked and advertise by means of 'me too' functionality. With continual copying and not much real innovation, there is little attention given to what the customers actually want. As the world quickly moves to an almost completely Web-based service model, the benefit to the user becomes the number one focus and priority.

The reality is setting in that the market for software will no longer tolerate the unbalanced cost vs. functionality dilemma. We think that the developments from the library vendors will have to go in the following direction:

- Reinvent outdated core software technology.
- Concentrate all efforts on speed and responsiveness.
- Clear distinction between back-end and web based front-end.
- Create attractive and user-friendly interfaces with a 'wow' factor.
- Simplify product functionality.
- Simplify business procedures and contracts.
- Limit (need for) documentation.

We see the possibility that only a part of the current ILS industry will be able to make the transition. As long as the library customer is placed at the top of the chain, there is a bright future for those ILS vendors who will embrace this new software paradigm and build a new suite of library services on top of it.

5. Conclusion

This is a similar story to our introduction, however, with an alternate ending. What we offer here is the possible future of the library from the perspective that search and accessibility are instantly achievable. 2007 and 2008: Information democracy, focus on search and accessibility, sources aggregation, quality stamp recognition, regional role, general world information – will all come together. By the same time, the value of the library will be reflected in the library's web identity. In the years of 2009 and 2010 the future will be with library vendors. While for the immediate period they will continue to compete by adding features and copying each other's developments, they will eventually catch up with the software companies outside of the library realm, those who are in 2006 moving out of the legacy model towards clever, innovative and user-focused development. The best ILS vendors will have made their transitions by 2010.

What does it take to get the people into the library? The public library could be recognized as a trustworthy and essential guide in the information landscape one can rely upon. The library's web identity will play a direct role in this recognition. By 2012, the physical libraries will be inspiring cultural environments that are recognized by everyone as a facilitator of life-long learning.

We strongly believe everyone involved within the library realm will take the responsibility and steps necessary to retain this invaluable tool for the future.

Search and web accessibility are key. Focus on the role of being the guide to information will lead to spending lots of energy and capital aggregating and opening up local and specialized resources – all in a single search. People will think of the library as their primary source of information; they will know how to find and access the content of the collections in- and outside the library, from any location, at any time. The users will finally demand something better, because they will suddenly realize they were becoming average and had nearly stopped

Introduction

questioning altogether. Library vendors will follow with innovative web-based solutions that answer the demands of the library users and information professionals.

Risen - Why Libraries Are Here To Stay

Information Democracy

The free availability of information is of supreme importance under democratic principles. The possibility of freely searching sources, to compare the quality of sources side by side, and of assessing and choosing what is most relevant to the user at that moment, is to exercise a right that belongs to the Key ideals of democracy. The library fulfills a role in communicating the idea that when you want to know something thoroughly, a walk among the different available sources is essential. To bring in the importance of the technology that is already available, you should be able to take that walk digitally as well. That is the power of the library that outweighs the value of only searching on the Internet. There must be a virtual consultation of the library, the collection, the books, the newspapers, the illustrated magazines, the relevant Internet websites, special collections, local cultural agencies, online book and music shops, and websites. Public libraries are able to perform such a role inherently. Who else or what other organizations could possibly fill this role of the library? Broad Internet searches will never be able to replace and perform and act as the public libraries do because that is one-sided, it is only part of what the library offers. Rather, the Internet can be a golden opportunity for the library to grasp and use as its port of entry for all of society.

Specialization is a core quality, which can accurately bind the community to the world around it so long as the collections are made accessible. This creates a distinction for the local library about which we seldom think. The information on the Internet is about broad, sweeping and generalized information for the masses. This has been created over time with the assumption that the more general it is, the more it will appeal to a wider audience. Conversely, however, it is the local library that can aggregate that specific set of quality sources, adding its own individual touches to it, making it more tailored and valuable to the community it serves.

> The library fulfills a role in communicating the idea that when you want to know something thoroughly, a walk among the different available sources is essential.

The great Mahatma Gandhi once said "Democracy must in essence... mean the art and science of mobilizing the entire physical, economic and spiritual resources of all the various sections of the people in the service of the common good of all." On another occasion he stated, "I have repeatedly observed that no school of thought can claim a monopoly of right judgment. We are all liable to err and are often obliged to revise our judgments." And he also said, "I attach the highest importance to quality irrespective almost of quantity... Numbers become irresistible when they act as one man under exact discipline. They are a self-destroying force when each pulls his own way or when no one knows which way to pull."

We live in an 'information democracy'. With a personal computer you can obtain copious amounts of publicly available information worldwide. Information you can get, but what about knowledge? Bill Gates wrote that most of the knowledge on which the so-called knowledge economy is based, "...is actually just information; data, facts and basic business intelligence. Knowledge itself is more profound." And he quotes management guru Tom Davenport, "Knowledge is information combined with experience, context, interpretation and reflection." There is an agreement between those gurus: quality (of knowledge) does not come with quantity (of information).

Gandhi touches on the ethics of information in that no one can claim a monopoly of 'right judgment' because everyone is prone to errors.

> "We are all liable to err and are often obliged to revise our judgments."

Gates suggests the development of software that 'watches' you discreetly while you are working and can make suggestions about related subjects or ideas. He suggests that even if the software makes a bad guess, "it could still be valuable in helping spark new ideas." Does this add to knowledge, can a software judge the context or one's personal experiences? What is the difference between a suggestion and a question? To help you invent (a question) seems more democratic than to steer your answers. Democracy, Gandhi says, has a responsibility: it teaches men and women to think for themselves.

Behind the Search Engines

Let us travel back in time to ancient Greece, which was the cradle of democracy. And let's have a look at Delphi where we could find Apollo's oracle in a cave on the slopes of Mount Parnassus. In its hey-day it was the most authoritative oracle in the Greek world. An 'oracle' is defined as a person or agency considered to be a source of wise counsel or opinion; an infallible authority, usually spiritual in nature. But was it? Were the answers to grave and lesser questions delivered in a democratic and proper fashion?

First, we were asking the gods and, as we know, Greek gods tended to be quite volatile. Their gods made their messages known to the people in many different formats. Second, there was Pythia, the oracle and medium who lived in a state of frenzy induced by hallucinogenic vapors rising from the chasm in her cave and in this state delivered the gods' messages in blurred words. Third, there were the priests – the 'prophetai' – who reshaped or interpreted her gibberish into enigmatic answers, which could lead you anywhere. 'Prophetes' means 'one who speaks on behalf of another person'.

The most famous instance of this comes down to us through a Delphic prediction given to Croesus, king of Lydia. In 550 BCE, Croesus was preparing to invade the Persian Empire when he consulted the Oracle about his chances for victory. After sacrificing 300 head of cattle to Apollo, he had gold and silver melted down into 117 bricks, which were sent to Delphi, along with jewels, statues, and a gold bowl weighing a quarter of a ton. With these gifts, Croesus sent his question of whether he should attack Persia.

The Pythia answered that, if he crossed a river, "Croesus will destroy a great empire." Encouraged by this response, he invaded Persia, only to suffer a decisive defeat. The Persians invaded and then conquered Lydia and captured Croesus, who thereafter bitterly denounced the Oracle. He sent his iron chains to Delphi with the question, "Why did you lie to me?" The Pythia correctly answered that her prophecy had been fulfilled. Croesus had destroyed a great empire — his own.

Whether right or wrong, it illustrates the weakness of this information chain. It challenges the veracity of the oracle and, by that, the veracity of the source; in this case, the gods. We could say that information was delivered in a hierarchical and, at the same time, non-committal way. And that was not only undemocratic, but also dubious and sometimes even dangerous.

> We could say that information was delivered in a
> hierarchical and, at the same time, non-committal way.

Today the oracle is the Internet, laden with information from all kinds of sources and the search engines are the 'prophetai', combining loose pieces of information and dumping them in front of us. We're guessing. Pick your choice. Could be this, could be that. Rather than usually offering us an answer to our questions, the search engine and the Internet tend to flood us with too much information, which can sometimes leave us worse off than we began.

The search engines reshape and interpret the Internet content into enigmatic answers. Nobody knows exactly how the answers are delivered. The gods behind the search engines can lead us anywhere.

The Library Tradition

Historically the library has always been a kind of 'information warehouse'. Western libraries appeared as early as 5th century BCE. The Royal Library of Alexandria, one of the oldest and possibly once the world's largest library, held literally everything it could seize. The early Western public libraries were established under the Roman Empire. Each succeeding Emperor strove to 'outdo' the previous one by expanding the collections as much as possible. Unlike the Greek Libraries, these were open to any readers and materials were kept on scrolls organized in one large room. This would become the world's first reading rooms.

Flashing forward, the 6th century CE saw the establishment of monasteries in Italy with libraries. Their purpose was to preserve both sacred and secular materials for future generations. Cassiodorus, who was a famous early librarian, not only built an extensive collection, but he also wrote many instructional texts aimed at monks on how to properly read, write, copy and preserve texts accurately. While most of these materials were later lost, Cassiodorus is one of the first documented 'unofficial Librarians' who attempted to create rules for librarianship. By the 8th century CE, Persia had imported the craft of paper making from China which lead to the popping up of hundreds of public libraries in most Islamic cities in the following century. Many of these libraries fell victim to wars over the centuries, however, several examples survived that continue to operate today.

The contents of many of the Islamic libraries were later copied by Christian monks in religious border areas and from there eventually made their way into Christian Europe. The accumulation of these works, across religious, linguistic and geographic realms eventually became the make-up of the modern library collections we know presently.

It has thus since become tradition that the library has held archives, records of business transactions, birth records and laws. The library was a source of all known information. Stories, ideas, theories, facts of nature and significant dates could all be found in the library. The library was also designed to cope with diversity. Any published item that the library could afford would theoretically go into its collection. The Library did evolve with society through the centuries, but for the most part, its role remained the same.

> The library was a source of all known information.

When the Library of Alexandria existed, a collection was primarily built by either taking items or having them created. It is said that King Ptolemy III of Egypt decreed that all visitors to the city were required to surrender all books and scrolls in their possession. These writings were then quickly copied by official scribes. The originals were put into the library and the copies were delivered back to the rightful owners. There were no questions asked, such was the level of power and control of the library back then. This may have helped to swiftly build what was estimated as a collection of tens of thousands of written works. An index or catalog of these holdings was never found and it is unclear how this collection was maintained or searched through.

The ancient library was also a center of research and study and would pay for items to be written, or factually verified. The library was responsible for ensuring validity of the knowledge it held and made available to the public.

Conflicting Powers

Since the very beginning, the printed work was the most important format for the library to preserve information. Printed works were first written on papyrus scrolls, later to be replaced with the codex, or the bound book as we know it today. As libraries developed, bound books were chained to their shelves to prevent theft, and in most libraries borrowing was out of the question.

Dating back to the Greek supremacy scholars held a high rank in the societal hierarchy. They heavily influenced collections by not only producing the works that filled the libraries, but also influencing what actually went into the collections through their power of knowledge. Society at that time held the library as the location or source of all knowledge. You knew then, that if you wanted to know something you went to the library to find it out. These beginnings show that even then, the library had a great marketing strategy, if even in a small way. Libraries were held in high esteem, they were for wealthy communities and cost much to maintain. However, the library's role as information warehouse was clear. Filled, organized and maintained by the people, the library was run on the basis of the democratic principle.

The librarians, those who maintained the collections to begin with, took on a very important role of ensuring the democratic significance of the collection and the perspective of the library itself. The librarians were the connection, the links between the library and the people. We feel that they still fulfill this role which is what will be argued further below. This democracy was of course derived on the principles established so famously by Greek society. But at the time, no one could look at a librarian and see the democracy happening. The librarians originated the first ways to build the collections in a manner that allowed quality information into the library without 'leaking' the quality. The librarians' connection to society was a force behind democracy.

The word "democracy" combines the elements demos (which means "people") and kratos ("force, power"). The so called 'classical democracy' became effective around 460 BCE, in the city-state of Athens. It is one of the very first known democracies, and probably the most important in ancient times. It was a unique and intriguing experiment in direct democracy where the people do not elect representatives to vote on their behalf but vote on legislation and executive bills in their own right. It is literally 'rule by the people, for the people'. Freedom of choice and freedom of speech were the most precious achievements of the early democracies. Never before had so many people spent so much of their time in governing themselves. It is – according to Aristotle – rule by the many, contrasting with the rule of the few (oligarchy) and the rule by a single person (autocracy).

> Freedom of choice and freedom of speech were the most precious achievements of the early democracies.

It is no coincidence that tragedy developed at the same time as democracy. Both assume personal freedom of choice. The hey-day of the tragedy (starting after 500 BCE) lasted not much longer than fifty years and was restricted to the city-state of Athens. It has had a great influence on European culture (and literature) and has had revivals thanks to playwrights including Shakespeare and Racine. Tragedy has its origins in festivities dedicated to the god Dionysius where dithyrambs (choric hymns) were sung by worshippers dressed in goat's skins (tragos).

Later an actor was placed opposite the chorus to act out the story. The playwright Aischylos (around 460 BCE) added a second actor and Sophocles later added another one in their plays. First the plays depicted mythological stories and later they referred to current events in Athens. The tragedy looks for a solution. Its structure is conflict, then bringing the conflict to a head and finally conflict resolution.

Aischylos provides an example to the above in his trilogy 'Oresteia', the story of the mythical Orestes who must kill his mother because she killed his father Agamemnon when he returned from Troy and found out she had a lover. Orestes flees in guilt and is haunted by the Erinyes, the goddesses of vengeance. He flees to Athens where the goddess Athena establishes a court (the Areopagos) in which the god Apollo acts in Orestes' defense. When there is a divided jury, Athena's pleads her support and he is freed in the end. By that, the 'Oresteia' is a mythological story and a reflection on and defense of the new (and vulnerable) democratic law system, which had been introduced in Athens around that time.

Thus, the tragedy reflects the proud, rational self-awareness of the Athenian citizens. The splendor of it is expressed by freedom, man's ability to determine his own destiny.

The works of the later playwrights Sophocles and Euripides show that the battle between fate and freedom is no longer fought between gods and mortals, but more and more on the human level. The role of the gods is restricted to the role we nowadays attribute to chance. In these later plays the context pointed more obviously to current events and to the flaws of political leaders. And some of the early democratic leaders, like Cleisthenes, sometimes acted as old-fashioned tyrants. If tragedy turned against anything, it turned against a political-ethical "all-or-nothing": an absolutism, which is the denial of limitation in the context of the need to be able to make choices. And limitation is exactly what tragedy wants us to see.

Classical tragedies are similar to each other by putting protagonists on the stage who struggle with a fundamental problem, often torn between conflicting powers. The circumstances create the context in which a hero (the protagonist) is carried away in an event, often with a monumental result. However, the outcome cannot be exclusively attributed to fate anymore. By his own miscalculation, blinded by his own right or recklessness, the tragic hero becomes part of these fatal events. Tragic heroes are confronted with tragic choices and feel responsible for them. However, this assumes that they have a certain freedom. Without freedom and responsibility, there is no tragedy.

The librarian, the protagonist

It is probable that the Internet only represents a small portion of the information and knowledge mankind has gathered since his beginning. The conclusion that can be drawn here is that if we use the Internet as our sole source when looking for real sets of trustworthy, relevant information, we leave everything to chance. The sheer amount of information on the Internet, our addiction to fast information and the ease with which a search engine can be accessed, all left as it stands, only provides for the fate of a mediocre world filled with average ideas. The libraries, their directors and information professionals, in their role of gathering information and making it accessible to the public, like the Greek heroes above, could be considered as the protagonists. To regain their position in the classic library tradition of the public information warehouse, they will be torn between conflicting powers. They will be confronted with 'tragic' choices within their positions to act freely. The library professional must now dare to stand up and be the protagonist; free, responsible and ready to fight mediocrity. Perhaps this will be a never-ending battle, but as long as the library professional perseveres, it will always remain a battle worth fighting.

> The libraries, their directors and information professionals, in their role of gathering information and making it accessible to the public, could be considered as the protagonists.

Today, the Information Professional is no longer called upon as the expert. We rely on algorithms and databases to organize and retrieve our information. We expect to gather information instantaneously through the Internet and we trust it. The information in the volumes that sit inside the library is disregarded, not because we believe it isn't factual, but because of the tediousness involved in searching for it. To read a book, or sift through journals, takes too much time. We move around the globe at faster speeds than ever before. With time being such a commodity, we view the library as an outdated place where it takes forever to find what we are looking for.

With the image of the library shrouded in an old-fashioned cloak, we have to look again at what it does and can offer. Perhaps the idea of the traditional Library needs to be reconsidered. The library still is the information warehouse, holding the keys to knowledge about our societies, but what if the library can not only compete with our need for faster information-gathering, but can use the very things that are closing our minds to it to help us change our views?

Web and Physical

We believe that both a change in the physical image of the library as well as the web identity is necessary to change societal views. In some cases, libraries are recognizing the importance of changing the physical appearance and image in order to bring patrons back to them. An example of one library that did so is the W.E.B. DuBois Library at the University of Massachusetts. DuBois Library redesigned its interior, moving thousands of books to storage, and installing lounge-like seating. They chose to adopt policies which have historically been forbidden such as allowing a coffee bar with food and the use of mobile phones. They made the library a place that the students wanted to be in, and it only benefited those students because they were no longer solely depending on a mouse click and an Internet search.

Many library users find it off-putting or are uncomfortable with walking over to a reference desk to ask a reference provider a question. Many more people simply do not want to ask for help because they may be embarrassed that they do not know how everything works in the library. A solution we have mentioned elsewhere in this book is one that DuBois Library has also implemented: instant messaging open on all computers. The user performs his search, and when he has a question about something, he just opens the message box, asks his question, and gets a direct response. This is being implemented in libraries eve-rywhere already. Most instant messaging software is free, making this a plausible solution for virtually any library and any kind of library. This also makes librarians and information providers more efficient because they too, do no have to leave their spots, and can help a number of pa-trons at the same time.

Many library users find it off-putting or are uncomfortable with walking over to a reference desk to ask a reference provider a question.

We found another example that was published in the U.S. Wall Street Journal of October 21, 2006. The Valparaiso University library, the Christopher Center, spent $33 million building a library twice as big as the old one, but with 80,000 fewer books. The book collection was replaced by open spaces, lounges, cafes and discussion areas. All of this was to get the students back into the library. They obviously accomplished this goal as the library is now completely full of students in comparison to two years ago when students couldn't even fit into the library. Library professionals allow food and drinks, they even encour-age conversation and they too are online available for students' online queries. This turned out to be a truly new evolution in library-thinking that flows in synch with the shift that needs to take place in web-think-ing.

"Back in my early days at Phoenix Public Library when I (Anthony) was a Clerk, I can remember an all-staff meeting that Toni Garvey, the City Librarian, had called to order. In this meeting she made references to the library's budget, how she worked to lobby for PPL and what the money could best be used for. At that time, the now famous building which had opened in 1995 still had a few unfinished areas. One of those areas was on the 4th floor, and it was in fact where the staff meeting was being held. The space was split; on one side the Arizona Room had just opened, and in the area where we sat, was what I had

come to believe would become the music room.

Coming from a family of musicians, and being one myself, I was very anxious to see the library's music collection receive its own dedicated area. Already, in my mind, there were so many possibilities of what could be done that would make music lovers and regular patrons alike, flow into that room. Toni Garvey broke my heart in that meeting. She made the announcement that the music room plan would be scrapped, and she had another idea for the space, and a long-term plan that would even put PPL on the map (again) as an innovator.

What Toni Garvey threw out as a concept back then, is now reality for Phoenix. The music room, a long forgotten memory, became the Teen Room. Simple enough, but actually what Toni and the administrative staff put forth was an idea that would turn the empty space into a completely innovative and much welcomed place for the teens of the Phoenix city center to come and feel right at home. Even more, nearly everything in the space was the idea of an actual teen. For the people, by the people.

Phoenix's Teen Room is an open-plan space with modern furnishings that both fit into the rest of the library's interior, and provide a youthful and progressive atmosphere. This is the place where kids come to browse through a collection meant for them, for them to listen to modern music, socialize with each other and the staff on the reference desk, and simply enjoy themselves. When something like this is put into effect, you don't promote it by telling any teen, "this is where you can come and do your homework." As anybody knows, teens will do the opposite of what you expect of them. No, instead, this place was billed as the "Starbucks for youth", the place in the library where noise is actually accepted by the staff, and the place where loitering is actually encouraged. The teens did their homework there completely of their own accord.

Risen - Why Libraries Are Here To Stay

Years after I had left PPL, moved to the Netherlands, and had started working with Medialab, I ran into Toni Garvey at an ALA conference. I don't know if she remembered my vocal protest to what was, to me, the slaying of the music room, but for whatever reason Toni immediately asked me if I had been back to see the finished Teen Room, and she invited me to tour it the next time I was passing through Phoenix. Well, I did, and I was a completely turned around, true fan from the moment I walked in. Mid-afternoon on a weekday, every lounge-like sitting surface was occupied by a young person. There was the sound of the latest radio-dance hit in the background. The layout, the lighting, the location of the reference staff, the whole area; impressed me well beyond my expectations. And you know what, I think even Toni Garvey and the PPL staff was that impressed as well. Because through years of planning, careful spending, great design, attention to detail and real use of user-feedback, they created the kind of space that got the kids back into the library.

Mid-afternoon on a week day, every lounge-like sitting surface was employed by a young person.

The Teen Room in Phoenix's main Burton Barr Library is so good that it not only inspired copies to be recreated in some of the branches, but other cities are coming to them for help building versions in their own libraries. And Phoenix did it AGAIN in the Children's department; fully catering to children's needs and desires to make their place theirs again.

So why was this important? Because ever since Internet access became as easy to come by as a water connection in your home, teens especially had become heavily reliant on simple web searches to gather the information they sought. The information wasn't just about where they could grab the latest concert tickets, or which new movie they wanted to see in the coming weekend, but especially with their school work. The library was *obsolete to the average teen because they would have to trek down to this building where they had to abide by library law (Shhh!), get lost in the stacks looking for something that they were interested in (Help!), and more importantly dig through endless information for stuff they could probably get right at home on their own computer. Right?*

Well, actually we know the library is filled to the brim with materials in the teen collection that is of the highest quality. The library is the place where reference providers are there to assist you to find what it is you're looking for. The library aggregates government documents, journals, periodicals, text books, encyclopedias, novels and websites all in one place. Oh, and did we mention that it's free?

So the Teen Room, perhaps sounding like a pretty simple idea here, was extremely important for Phoenix. It is also important for all public libraries, because in order for libraries to remain relevant to their communities, they will have to keep up. They will have to offer the kind of environments their local communities need and desire in order to keep the people coming. And at the end of the day, the library exists as a public service, so it is its responsibility to actually serve the public.

I am not longing for Phoenix to have a music room anymore. I was a teen user of the Phoenix main library and I wish I could have had such a place to hang out, do my homework, speak to teen-friendly librarians and find what I wanted all in one place. Phoenix Public Library's Teen Room is a perfect example of how libraries around the world need to stop spending large amounts on shifting their collections around, or purchasing off-beat software that doesn't make anybody happy, or buying outdated reference materials that cost thousands of dollars and no one uses, and start redefining their images as a place where people go. This is one more step in ensuring how the public library will survive."

Libraries that achieve a change in their physical image are putting forth a 'hipper' appearance. While this is another way for the library to remain relevant, we feel that the web accessibility and web identity are still key factors. Even those libraries that are updating their interior design, when you look closely at their nicely designed and user-friendly web interfaces, are still missing certain key aspects. What is often missing is the true aggregation of sources. Or the ability to search and browse right from the homepage. You often need to dig deep to get in touch with the collections. When you go to a nicely designed site, you are able to look past a few extra tabs than are actually necessary. But when you do a 'general' search, you realize that the search being performed is covering about ⅓ of what resources the library has available. So does this mean in order to truly see every source, you have to re-search your term(s) multiple times?

The quality information that only libraries can offer must be fully web accessible. Searching the aggregated set of hybrid sources must be an easy process. And the web image of the library must be that it is a modern online location that people will go to and clearly view as an alternative to simply performing an Internet search. In fact, a library search should be just as easily accessible and as immediately thought of as an Internet search!

The Forgotten Role of the Library

> "The changing faces of libraries, revolutionary changes in the physical forms of information sources, novel methods in information storage and retrieval, application of information technology and communication technology in libraries opened up a number of new challenges in the library profession."
>
> — G. Devarajan - Head of Department of Library and Information Science, University of Kerala.

Information Democracy

What has happened to the library in the past 50 years could be seen as a digression, rather than a progressive evolution. The image of the library is that it has failed to keep up with the needs and desires of society. The library is no longer the center of information for society, but instead information has spread everywhere and become available to anyone through new technologies. This, in turn, makes information vulnerable. Where the library can control and manage sources of information, sources on the Internet have no guardian. The library became an outdated entity because it remained wholly focused on the catalog of printed materials. Where the library did succeed in advancing, it failed to market its services to the public, to let people know what it actually offered. This provoked society to seek newer and faster ways of retrieving information. They were tired of waiting for the library, so they went after the information themselves. The library's role in society as the central information conductor was forgotten and certainly not pursued.

This lack of relevance in society pulled the library away from its ancient role and allowed it to be left by the wayside. This is both the fault of society, seeking ever faster ways of retrieving and communicating information, and of the library for not conveying a message back that it too, still had a vital role to play.

Outside the library, technology advanced from simple electronic data storage to the personal computer and networking becoming readily available to nearly anyone. The library did not anticipate the escalation of companies such as Microsoft or Google making access to information so open or common. Of course, within the libraries there were progressive library personnel who wanted to instill change and evolve using everything the technological market could offer. But overall, the library as an entity remained stuck on a treadmill, completely concentrated on internally automating its catalog and maintaining the collection. When the Internet took shape as a virtual world at the end of the 1990s, the library did not take advantage of what we then coincidentally called the 'information highway': to give the public easy access to the catalog and the collections from anywhere. Instead, the library continued the internal path of self-organization and collection main-tenance. How did the library get so complicated? While the librarians were busy discussing MARC, Z39.50, Open Archives Standards and Authority Control, the Internet public was simply saying: Search and Find.

> "Overall, the library as an entity remained stuck on a treadmill, completely concentrated on internally automating its catalog and maintaining the collection.

Throughout the last 20 years the library continued its focus on the automation of the collection through adapting the Online Public Access Catalog (OPAC)*, but throughout this time, the basis was still the original card catalog. Focus was not placed on the public access to the catalog, but rather continuous internal development. What access the public had to the catalog, was only to the catalog itself and not to any other resources.

Revolution in the Access to Information

The discrepancy between the library and the outside world grew throughout the 1990s. Today, technology is evolving at a faster rate than ever before and the Internet has developed into its own artificial world, containing the theories, languages, images, history and concepts of the world. Communication of information has been at the heart of this advancement with humans daily upgrading the way they share their knowledge and communicate with each other.

Beyond the computer, the mobile telephone is fast becoming the smaller laptop computer replacement. Mobile phones offer technology beyond making calls such as taking photos, accessing e-mail, accessing the Internet, sending and receiving news alerts, instant messaging and blogging. Mobile phones and mp3 players are now used to download

Information Democracy

spoken word books, pod casts, arrays of images, photo collections and all manner of training courses. All of this is based on the need to retrieve information efficiently, without being tied to a book, a cable, or even a viewing screen. Technology is now geared towards usability – building ways and means for anyone to gather information anywhere.

So why does it seem that the library is so rigidly opposed to using these technological advancements to its benefit, rather than try to compete with them? If these are the means people are using to gather information outside of the library, why couldn't they be used to gather it inside? The theory returns to the theme of the library having been so focused on internal automation before they even look at public access to the collection. The OPAC is not user friendly to those without a Master's degree in Library Science, nor is it designed or styled in a way that people are expecting. This makes the reference provider burdened by every patron coming into the library looking for material because they simply cannot use the OPAC themselves. Or, the patrons have no desire to use the old-fashioned, grueling DOS-like, drop-down menu filled, gray, option-laden screen layouts.

> The OPAC is not user friendly to those without a Master's degree in Library Science, nor is it designed or styled in a way that people are expecting.

The librarian who is so familiar to the difficult-to-use and unfriendly interfaces of the current OPAC standard is fine with them because it was, after all, an improvement over their card catalog. Besides, why shouldn't a patron come to them for questions to be answered? All librarians know the classification systems by memory, and know everything in their collections.

It becomes more of a question of image than it does truth. The internally focused library failed to send out the message that it was indeed evolving and bringing these technologies to the fingertips of the patrons. Instead, the patrons who were loyal to the library were able to take advantage of them, and the rest of the world did not get 'the memo'. It was only much more recently that libraries saw the need to promote the internal technological advances that have been going on for some time now, just in order to stay open.

This societal revolution in the access to information has made the library a dinosaur. The image of the library is based upon the question: Why should someone trek to the library to find information and be reliant on the librarian when it is available nearly anywhere? You need only turn on your PC, enter a few words, and the answers you are looking for come up instantly before your eyes. The library is just full of dusty old books anyway, right?

The Five Laws of Library Science

Michele V. Cloonan and John G. Dove wrote an article on Ranganathan's ideology of librarianship, entitled "Ranganathan Online" which appeared in the Library Journal, April 1, 2005. In their article they make several points that not only support the argument for the Information Democracy, but clearly show the relevance of Ranganathan's original words from the 1960s to the state of the library today.

To start, let's have a look at S.R. Ranganathan's Laws:

1. Books are for use.

2. Every reader his or her book.

3. Every book its reader.

4. Save the time of the reader.

5. A library is a growing organism.

Cloonan and Dove feel there is little hindering the library from upholding the Five Laws in the electronic age. Their article argues that libraries simply need to offer a real alternative to consumer-based search engines that were never intended to replace the library, but are. These search engines are doing so because today's 'information consumer' is looking for the fastest and easiest way to gather their information. As Cloonan and Dove state, "…e-resources often remain hidden from the user. Our reliance on consumer-focused search engines leaves whole portions of the web inaccessible…" The issue here is that by using Internet Search engines, they are not getting the best information because they are not looking past the first page of results, and the results that do appear on the first page are there based on popularity and payment for placement there.

Cloonan and Dove's conclusion here is that this kind of information is not false, but it cannot be compared equally to the kind of quality information that the library can offer.

The information a library is responsible for holding and maintaining is based on a community's needs, and not the consumer market's desires. This information should also be expected to follow a coherent format. The Internet cannot be described as coherent because the information is portrayed in virtually any form, language and perspective imaginable. While the Internet's offerings are diverse enough to offer something for everyone, there is little or no organization whatsoever of the Internet.

Where the library collection is organized and structured to ensure access by anyone to the information found in it, the Internet is like a wall of graffiti that has been painted over time and again. Somewhere in the graffiti is a message, with no real intended audience, no reference date and often no established author.

The value of the local library is probably the most overlooked of all. The local library is the responsible source for information that pertains to an individual community, with its own identity. The local library that caters to the needs of its patrons offers more than reference books, but also access to local culture, events, news, background information, opinions, politics and lifestyle in a perspective that an unfamiliar library could never give. Where an Internet search's top down view of the world can give a global reference of Internet web pages, no other source can give a window into a community like a local library.

An Internet search engine conveys results from the Internet from a top-down, Delphi-like, 'big brother' perspective. This makes it undemocratic. Broadly searching on the Internet does not ensure that you will find the best, most reliable and most relevant information. The library world is starting to realize what it takes to offer the best quality information to the public. The aggregation and integration of sources into a single, user-friendly search – one which is unfiltered and based solely on relevancy and not on popularity is necessary to allow the library to democratize information supply.

> The local library is the responsible source for information that pertains to an individual community, with its own identity.

The Information Democracy is a concept meaning that the best information is always what a person seeking information should be striving to find. The best information is what the library should consider its highest priority to carry and maintain. This concept is exactly as it is named: democratic. Information gathered by the library could be done so by totally radical means. Rather than only relying on traditional means, sources or formats, libraries should allow active participation from their communities. Online panels, local forums and blogs can be facilitated, hosted and opened up next to the catalog and subscripted sources. The idea that the library is the guardian of a community's information does not have to mean the library is the only say in what is factual, or even the best information. We see the library as the focal point of local, relevant, trustworthy information that allows and encourages participation and discussion.

Where traditional means of gathering information, particularly as it has been for the last several centuries would mean relying solely on academia for proof of fact and truth before the information could be shared; radical means would mean looking beyond academia, directly to the community. Experts on various topics that give insight to the library are an invaluable resource, and by using technology, it is much easier to communicate this information. The library still remains as the 'verifier' of the information, and in turn, becomes the access point.

Regional perspective

Using the available modern technological advances mentioned earlier, the library can benefit from input from the community through simple and easy means. More and more, blogs are becoming common place, not only for individuals but also for institutions, companies, schools, libraries, etc. There are library fans, patrons and general users that are using their own blogs to promote the library's collection, to praise and even to criticize the library. Furthermore, the library is receiving support from community experts on various subjects as an added resource to what the library physically holds in its own collection. And in fact, local periodicals, both printed and digital, already represent the communities' invaluable sources. It now only makes sense to allow the library to be the one to collect, aggregate and offer these all together at once.

This community input makes the information a library carries more democratic because it involves people in an inclusive manner, rather taking librarianship in the same top-down perspective that an Internet search would, it provides for those (often tax-paying or tuition paying) patrons to have the chance to enhance the library. The library is the only (often government) institution in society that can freely offer such an open inclusion and only benefit from it, rather than suffer. As it remains the library's duty to verify all the information it receives, the library can only be enriched by such input from its own community.

Beyond the Web, the library gatherer and caretaker of information can look at all formats and offer a localized perspective that a general Internet search cannot. By creating specific collections in a city or region that is composed of local expertise on something relating to that specific area, the library becomes the expert on that subject. The library becomes the authoritative source on that subject. Only the library can collect, verify and make information accessible from a regional perspective with the truth in mind, and in a manner not achievable by an outside source. This responsibility to 'protect' a local perspective and 'own' local information on a local subject is what the library professionals must begin to realize as their greatest task, adding their neutrality, expertise and putting their own 'library quality stamp' on that information.

> By creating specific collections in a city or region that is composed of local expertise on something relating to that specific area, the library becomes the expert on that subject.

By placing this emphasis on local information expertise, the library not only gives its community the best resource available, but also, as any public library can work with other communities through online means, that local library can now offer the world its expertise. There is no limit. And why shouldn't information be emerging from the best resource? That is what makes the difference between a top-down perspective in information, such as performing a broad Internet search with a search engine, and providing a bottom-up perspective with the very best sources, those closest to any given subject, verifying it all factually, then making it available to the world via their own site. With nearly all libraries in the world now online, one can search every community's single catalog (or a cooperation of local catalogs in a coalition of libraries) for the best information there is.

The Hybrid Library Network

Taking the concept from the bottom to the top, a network of local libraries would be an invaluable design in that the first-handed source information would be passed on from community to community, from town to city to state to nation. The information in a small-town library would be just as available to a national library, however, giving that small town library the direct responsibility for information management ensures that even the broader perspective does not get diluted.

The concept of libraries locally collecting and openly sharing their collections is not a new concept, it is simply a much overlooked one. The information in libraries' collections is there, but it is so commonly 'misplaced' or access to it is obscured. Libraries today even have the desire to hybridize their collections, sharing not only more modern formats, including qualified websites, but sharing their entire catalogs, opening access to information in an 'umbrella' approach with the vast web information now verified and factual, as we expect and demand of our libraries.

The information in a 'Hybrid Library Network' becomes user-specific and completely adaptable. The library becomes the 'hybrid' source in this case because of the flexibility to offer information from print to digital formats, from local to global perspective, all at once, without fear of dilution or falseness.

"Libraries are selective, while the Internet's main value is its lack of selectivity," as stated from Wisconsin Librarian blog meaning that the need for Information Democracy in society is real. This reflects back once again to the role of the tragic protagonist fighting mediocrity in his freedom to select and make choices. Even if libraries had unlimited space and budgets they would not purchase and offer everything that exists purely because it exists. The role of the library is to combine the free access with selecting what is the best information for the targeted public. "Every library has its public, every public has its library."

The library could retake its position as the leading information provider to society if society had just as easy, if not better access to the information it holds. Today, web based technology is readily available to make this real. Web based intelligent search and indexing technologies are the weapons and armor for the library's protagonist on his quest against fate, chance and mediocrity.

> "Every library has its community, every community has its library."

Technology that has taken the library's power away is now giving it back – in ways never before imagined. The library, risen from the ashes, becomes a modern network of the best, most advanced tools, accessing the best quality information out there, with the modern networked public in mind. You see, the library does verify and update all of its holdings. But it aggregates and integrates other relevant sources at the same time, only with a neutral, quality focused, democratic feel. The modern library isn't just a superior source of information; the modern library is owned by the people and is for the people. It's the public that gets to shape how the library evolves from here.

The Information Democracy prohibits the death of ideology, which would allow our information and knowledge to become average and mediocre. It combats the mechanisms that create the illusion of free will and evenly distributed information. It is one more organ in information acquisition that must be included in the mix in order to ensure the sustainability and bettering of the public library as a real and important entity in our societies.

Search and Accessibility

Mnemosyne was beautiful. She was a Titaness, a daughter of Ouranos, the sky, and Gaia, the earth. We don't know much about her, but what we know we haven't forgotten, thanks to her.

This is why.

Zeus, a son of the Titans himself, fell in love with Mnemosyne 'of the beautiful hair' and, knowing Zeus, he got what he wanted. The myth tells that before Hera became his wife, he laid with Mnemosyne for nine nights. As a reward he let her discover the power of reason, and he enabled her to designate the names of objects, thereby being the bringer of words and language, which would help mortals to communicate with each other. And more than that, she could also give mortals the power to remember, a gift upon which many talents depend. Mnemosyne is the classic goddess of Memory.

She gave life to nine daughters: Calliope – the heroic epic and philosophy, Clio – the history, Melpomene – the tragedy, Euterpe – music and pleasure, Erato – erotic poetry, Terpsichore – dance and lyric poetry, Thalia – comedy, Polymnia – rhetoric and sacred songs and Urania – astronomy. We mortals call them the Muses.

The story of Mnemosyne and her children probably symbolizes the desired ingredients for culture, for civilization and by that – we dare say – collective knowledge. They represent what we know and why we know each other. And, in fact, they represent the first classification system for human knowledge. Through the millennia we have built temples for the Muses ('museum' is the derivate of the Greek 'mousaion', the place of the Muses), places where the disciplines and talents could meet. And – interestingly – the famous Library of Alexandria and its circle of scholars were formed around a 'mousaion', built by Ptolemy I, a general under Alexander the Great. Everything humanity knew at that point in history was collected, written down, categorized, maintained and made accessible by librarians. Knowledge was searchable and accessible for those who wanted to know, and, admittedly, were of a class allowed to know.

> Through the millennia we have built temples for the Muses, places where the disciplines and talents could meet.

By the beginning of the Christian era the Library of Alexandria had been destroyed, but other libraries followed its example and they went on collecting, categorizing and maintaining these new temples of knowledge. Some libraries did this for the better, some for worse. Some were more accessible, and some less.

Think of the Benedictine monks in Umberto Eco's 'The Name of the Rose' where the protagonists – the Franciscan friar William of Baskerville and his young apprentice – explore a labyrinthine library in a mysterious abbey where a murder has been committed. More unexplainable murders follow.

However, thanks to his powers of logic and deduction William succeeds in solving the murders and the mysteries of the abbey and her hidden treasures, including discovering Aristotle's book on Comedy. William demonstrates the power of deductive reasoning. He refuses to accept the diagnosis of 'demonic possession' despite demonology being the traditional explanation. By keeping an open mind, collecting facts and observations, following intuition and didactic reasoning (with his apprentice), he makes decisions as to what he should investigate. Not only does Eco's story coincidentally involve libraries and librarians, but it demonstrates the crucial importance of chance in any investigative endeavour. Though William's theorized solutions do not always match the actual events, he could not have solved the abbey's mysteries without them.

Human knowledge has become more complex through the ages and, therefore, so has the finding of the right answers to questions. Accessible knowledge and the power of reasoning is an important determinant in the outcome. Bare information that can be browsed and placed in a context can become knowledge. It plays an important role in both interpretation and judgement. Still, sometimes it seems difficult to find, either stashed away or drifting on the World Wide Web, other online sources and in library collections. But if it isn't Mnemosyne and her daughters, who can be blamed?

Sweet mission statements

Most public libraries have the ease of access to their collections stated in their mission statements.

> "The Mission of The Free Library of Philadelphia, USA is to provide to all segments of Philadelphia's diverse population a comprehensive collection of recorded knowledge, ideas, artistic expression and information in a variety of media, including current technology; to assure ease of access to these materials; and to provide programs to stimulate the awareness and use of these resources."

A living example of Mnemosyne and the Muses at work.

> "It is the mission of the Guilderland Public Library to select, acquire, organize and preserve books and other materials of contemporary interest and permanent value for the education,

enjoyment and intellectual stimulation of the entire community. The Library strives also to guide young people toward a love of reading and an awareness of books and other library materials as a means of satisfying their needs and interests."

If we look in Singapore, Scandinavia, South America, or nearly anywhere around the world, a similar mission of public libraries is echoed repeatedly.

The library collections, both physical and digital are always maintained and offered with the utmost care. However, despite this fact, actual usage of these knowledge sources is a mere fraction of the usage of the Internet for finding information. Yes, in the back of our minds, we do want the library to continue to play a vital role in information facilitation. Yes, subconsciously, we do all know that the most obvious way to achieve an increase in usage of the collection must come by giving better access to it through the same Internet. And yes, we have realized that we need to move away from what has been such a focus for so many years: cataloging and collection development. The movement will be towards the accessibility and attractiveness of the collection through the Web, towards visions, technologies and products that make the search process more attractive. But they are only just being discovered and recognized as attainable means and methods.

So we believe the public library is already the guardian of information, the realm and protectorate of the information democracy. Yes, it IS powered by dedicated people committed to serving the greater public good, filled with validated facts, diverse opinions, a multitude of qualified resources, a wide array of potential useful technologies and the flexibility and intelligence to cope with our need to have information instantly and conveniently.

If the public library wants to continue to play a vital role in information facilitation, then it would appear that the most obvious way to achieve an increase in usage of the collection must come by using the Internet to improve access to their collections. An intelligent is move towards the accessibility and attractiveness of the collection through the Web. The Internet must no longer be viewed as a competitor to the library, but rather as a tool to be used to the library's advantage.

The new focus of the library on search and accessibility services, technologies and products will make the search process more intelligent, more user-oriented and more attractive. Search technologies that can aggregate sources and offer it all in ONE single interface are already available today. Knowledge that once was freed by the Muses is now brought to the public by the library's web search environment.

Liberate the collection

Positive intentions are there. We're all heading in the right direction. Our visions are clear. It is just the ability to act, and overcoming the fear to change that are limiting us in our capabilities. Most people do not like change, and the image of the stuffy old library is not for naught. The library historically has tried to 'protect' its collections from the outside forces that could harm all that information. So it's no wonder why libraries are that bit slower than many other institutions to accept changes, whether they are in management style, technology, processes or even physical design.

First, we need to agree on the fact that the accessibility and facility of search through the library's web access plays a crucial role in the survivability of the library. Public libraries simply must have websites to allow their patrons to get in touch. Academic libraries must have websites to allow their students to connect to the range of sources. The whole world is web based and linked together. We're all Skyped and MySpaced and Flickred and Blogged. If we are all about publicly sharing information and communicating, where are the libraries in all of this?

Once access is established, it is then the issue of how easy it is for the visitor to search the collection. How close is it to the search methodology they already know from the Internet, and how attractive is it for the library visitor to get (virtually) inside.

We believe there is a big opportunity for the library here. Why? There is a lot of room for implementing modern intelligent search technologies that are intrinsically better than the existing Internet search systems. Today, search technologies are available that take existing web search concepts as their starting point, while intelligently improving the search process, making full use of the available knowledge that is hidden in quality databases and other connected sources. Presumptions that exist: databases must be rich and full of meta-data and meta-information (catalog: yes, websites: no) and technology must be able to extract and use the knowledge that is hidden in the sources fully and automatically. Both presumptions can be found within the library realm, while outside this realm, on the Internet, either presumption is difficult to come by.

> Today, search technologies are available that take existing web search concepts as their starting point, while intelligently improving the search process, making full use of the available knowledge that is hidden in quality databases and other connected sources.

However the premise in most existing search systems for digital collections is that the user expects to find the right answer to their questions right away. Lots of energy, effort, research and money is spent on building systems that should work according to this premise. Most OPAC search interfaces offer the web user a screen with fields like Title, Author or Subject to make the search easier. And the use of a 'Boolean expression' is basically what this is all about too. Users try to formulate one syntax question that contains all the pre-knowledge that they have in order to find the answer. Then the question is sent to the system, the system processes it, and after a while the system returns with the answer that matches the question, with the most relevant answers, as they are calculated by the search algorithm, ranked on top. This is basically the way most search systems work.

We feel that this idea, the concept that Internet search engines should work in this manner is a gigantic error in theory. Here is a metaphorical story that explains why.

One early morning a wise man took some of his students for a walk in the countryside. The forests and fields and all the flowers were covered with dew. After a short while the sun rose and the dewdrops sparkled brilliantly. It was a feast for the eyes. The old man stopped by a large dewdrop and gathered his students around it without obstructing with the light of the sun. And he asked them which colour the dewdrop was.

"Red", said the first one, "Orange", said the second one. "Yellow", the third, "Green", the fourth, "Blue", the fifth and the sixth said "Violet". They were quite surprised about the difference and because every one of them thought he had seen the true colour, they reached a point where they almost started to quarrel. The old master let them change places a few times and slowly they realised that each of them had spoken the truth in spite of their different observations. After some time, the wise man told all the students to return where they had previously been standing. However, now the sun had moved to another position in the sky, and so the dewdrop reflected entirely different colours.

New intelligent search systems attempt to grasp the moral of this story. They are based on interaction with the user, making search a process rather than a single action. The interaction is derived from the context and associations, different meanings, suggestions and ideas the user will have along the way.

Modern, intelligent search systems play the role of asking the questions during the process to help the user along during his quest for information. It can do so by giving the user the suggestions, alternatives and variations described earlier, while providing the connection to an array of available knowledge.

New intelligent search systems are based on interaction with the user, making search a process rather than a single action.

At the same time, the output of the search process, in a modern intelligent search system, will automatically rank the result set from the users' perspective or angle. Mind the position of the students watching the colours of the dewdrops. When the user receives a couple of hundred results related to his search term, an intelligent system should be able to offer the user the ability to take different 'positions' in order to re-rank and re-shuffle the result set towards the position the user wants (or has) at that very moment.

Classic search

Let's face it, users simply cannot find everything of valuable relevance in a first search based on their own pre-existing knowledge. This is a key reason why the classic method of searching (one question-to-one answer) is problematic.

The classic search process assumes the user knows exactly what he is looking for. For example, the user is looking for a specific edition of a book by a particular author. Presumably the search system would place this book as the very first item in the search result list. But an intelligent search system would also give suggestions and hints to other formats, such as CDs, books-on-tape, other works by that author, and even related books about the same subject. These are all items the seeker may or may not know exists. The user's pre-existing knowledge of that one edition of that particular book may limit how he will search. The fact is he may be interested in other works by the author, or even related works by other authors, but the search system may not display any of these items to him. This is why we believe a search system should always support the user's pre-existing knowledge while enriching his query formulation, even when the user knows exactly what he is looking for.

Search and Accessibility

There is also the situation where a user is not certain about what he is looking for. In fact we believe this pertains to most users. A user may type a search term that is in the area of what he is looking for, and he is hoping to find specific material on that subject, but does not know what exists or what is available. In this case, suggestive search systems are the key to unlocking a path for the user, while allowing the user to choose his search path towards the sources of information that are directly related to what he wants.

The final problem with classic search systems is that semantics and language are simply too complicated in structure to pose a question perfectly. Language alone simply contains too many variations to allow for this. The perfect (single) question that leads to the perfect (single) answer is non-existent.

This is why we believe a search system should always support the user's pre-existing knowledge while enriching his query formulation, even when the user knows exactly what he is looking for.

To support the case for intelligent, suggestive search systems, we spoke to someone with a history of involvement in the field who has always had a unique perspective and opinion on search.

Professor Thijs Chanowski is the original founder of Medialab, a former research laboratory of Philips on software development and research on semantics and intelligent search algorithms. Today Medialab has transformed into Medialab Solutions B.V., headquartered in Amsterdam, and producer of the AquaBrowser search solutions for Libraries.

Professor Chanowsky retired in 2005. In the Netherlands, he was known as one of the initial producers of 'De Fabeltjeskrant', or Fables Newspaper, an immensely popular children's educational program which aired from 1968 until 1992. Among many other things, he was involved in the development of the world's first optical laser disk for

Philips, and was a department chair at the University of Amsterdam as the professor in multi-media and communication.

Chanovski lives in a small village called Schellinkhout, behind a dike next to the Dutch IJsselmeer. All the typical images you can conjure up of the Dutch landscape can be found here. This area is rich in greenery with the stone dike barriers holding back the water from the farmland, creating the below-sea level polder area, and filled with nature, dairy cows and quaint village cottages. He has his own particular view on search.

"Most search systems of today are based on existing previous knowledge. Basically, the quality of the result of the search process depends on the pre-knowledge of the user. The quality of the search process depends on the user's ability to formulate quality alternative search terms that will bring him closer to the answer; or his ability to use a specific vocabulary or a set of rules that is used by the search engine.

> "Most search systems of today are based on existing previous knowledge. Basically, the quality of the result of the search process depends on the pre-knowledge of the user."

Search systems tend to use the old search paradigm: previous knowledge-based and relevance-based. Most people are still looking for the search system that will give the single true answer on the single formulated true question. They want systems that seek the absolute truth. The logic behind this is founded on the old mathematical era of databases and structures. Every subject is stored in a labelled bin and the structure is the key element to finding the stored items again and again. We all know from our own experiences in creating folders and directories on our computer desktops, that this is an illusion.

Then there is the problem of the language itself. Language is unreliable. First you have the misspellings. Everybody makes them, it's a human error. There are still so many search systems that cannot cope with that. When you make a spelling mistake, the systems do not make you aware of it. Some systems now start helping you with "did you mean" and then mentioning the right term. This, at least, is a huge improvement. Aluminum vs. aluminium. Tsjaikowski vs. Tchaikovsky. Just check on Google. Both terms will give a completely different result set. The information is in there, but the system doesn't bother to alert the user. It is built on retrieving exact data. I have a collection at home of 23 different spellings of my own name."

Note: Did you notice the different spellings of his name at the beginning of this section?

The Professor continues, "Words have different meanings, or even opposite explanations depending on where you are. To illustrate what I mean, have you heard the funny story of Nasreddin? He often appears as a whimsical character of a large Persian medieval folk tradition of short stories, which resemble Zen stories. Nasreddin sat on a riverbank when someone shouted to him from the opposite side: "Hey! How do I get across?" "You are across!" Nasreddin shouted back.

I see that there are several ways of how we can make technology work for the user. They are all based on query enrichment. Any item someone searches is enriched with relevant items or information. The items that are used to enrich the query must all be related to the actual content. So, they must be derived form the content itself by intelligent algorithms. Some systems make use of man-made enrichments, a bit more like thesauri. Although they will serve a certain purpose in some circumstances, I do not believe those systems will keep on working. They are relying on ongoing maintenance. I propose that only fully automated enrichment query algorithms will keep working."

"The items that are used to enrich the query must all be related to the actual content."

So what kinds of possibilities are there? If someone is looking for 'pancake', for example, within the basic ILS based search systems, the user will have to know in which query box he enters the term 'pancake'. Title, subject?

With the familiar Internet search engines you need only to enter 'pancake' into one query box. This is already an improvement. Instead, the problem here is that you usually receive 10,000 search results in the broadest manner. These search engines only search on the text string 'p-a-n-c-a-k-e'. Any time that string appears in the database, it will be retrieved. And the more often it appears in a result, the higher the result will be ranked. In many cases this will be a much too broad correlation so of those 10,000 results, you must sift through and decide what is relevant to your search and what is not. This is always a daunting task. It would be nice if the system actually helped you sort through these results and made the process easier, but there is no intelligence in the search. The search algorithm does not take the meaning or context of 'pancake' into account.

How would we begin to describe a modern, intelligent, context based search system that can and does take some of the possible meanings (semantics) into account?

The system would enrich the search term with a set of items (broadening terms) that might have to do with what the user wants to find. There are several possibilities modern technologies are able to generate, coming from the content or from other existing meta-sources, all by themselves. So be aware: all suggested terms, query enrichments, etc., are coming from the content somewhere. This means there can never be any dead-ends. On every enriched item, there must be a search result in the information. This even implies that when a misspelling appears as a result, it's because the misspelling appears somewhere in the data.

Now let's try to summarize what Professor Chanowski means. Queries are enriched with words from the existing content that are in some way related to the search terms. Here are a couple of examples of how such relationships can be made:

Search and Accessibility

Permissiveness: pankake, panncake, pancakes, panbake

With permissiveness, we allow the user to make mistakes. This is the familiar "Did you mean...?" phrase that pops up in many modern search systems. But, permissiveness also means that the user is made aware of the fact that the information contains results that are close to your search term, but only spelled a bit differently. An intelligent system should recognize these terms on the fly. For instance, the reaction could be something like: "Hey, you are looking for pancake? The nicest recipe has been put somewhere by someone who misspelled pancake." Or, "You will find the best information in an article called 'All about pancakes.'"

This is what we call permissiveness. In our daily lives, human communication is based on it. We are very permissive with each other. Why should a system be any different?

Semantics: pancake, crepe, pizza.

When does a pancake stop being a pancake and become a thick crepe or a thin pizza? This has to do with semantics, the meaning of the word pancake. Language is so unreliable! You may be looking for a pancake, but having a vision of a nice thin crepe in your mind. The content may contain the best information about crepes, while you are searching with the term pancake. An intelligent search system should make you aware of this. "Hey, you are looking for pancake, but what about a nice crepe?" Again, in normal life and communication between humans, this is the way we behave. We communicate, exchange and discuss ideas and we place strong emphasis on the meaning of the words we are using. Search systems should (at least try to) do the same.

Context: breakfast, dinner, kitchen, nice flavour and smell, recipe, syrup, bacon.

Any search term we use will get its full meaning in the context of who we are, where we are, what we are looking for. The search is enriched enormously and the relevance of the result set is greatly increased by adding the context of the original term. Are we looking for pancake in the context of a breakfast food? Or are we looking for additionally related items like bacon and syrup. When the system points out to the user that the sources contain items, like syrup and bacon, which have relationships with pancake, these items will be ranked much higher in relevance than another item, even if it contains the word pancakes 26 times. In real life, all our observations are colored by the context. When a pancake becomes a part of a child's definition of breakfast, the smell of freshly baked pancakes adds to the good feeling. The context enriches the pancake and makes it, in this context, part of breakfast.

Domain: flour, yeast, enzymes, milk

The domain speaks for itself. When searching for a subject, you enter a specific domain. The term is always related to its domain in any situation. There will never be pancakes without their ingredients, flour and milk. It might be helpful for the user if the system could indicate which elements of the search term's domain are hidden in the sources as well. This type of knowledge is very relevant, although not always on the surface. Often, this type of information only becomes relevant when it is missing. In the middle of making breakfast you run out of milk. After a quick rush to the store, the domain is again complete.

Search is a process. When you know exactly what you are looking for, the search system should give you the right set of answers right away. But in many cases you do not know the best way to pose the query, what term you should use. Even when you search a generic term like 'gardening' the system wouldn't know if you were looking for gardening in the context of architecture, landscape, garden design, photography, green houses, history or climate zones. Or even which edition, which language or format you would like to retrieve. A modern, intelligent search system will make the user aware of this meaning, triggered by the user's search term. "Oh, I meant the Backyard Book by Tricia Foley. I didn't know this was available as well!" A search system should help you find the most relevant context and set of answers. The system will help and direct you on the way. It is a process of scatter and gather. One may be looking for the needle in the haystack, but finding the milk maid instead. We could call this the 'Zen of Search'.

> A modern, intelligent search system will make the user aware of this meaning, triggered by the user's search term.

You begin, as is the case in most searches, by entering the search terms you understand to be relevant to your search. The process results in suggestions of known associations of your terms in order to give you a chance to steer the search. The associations come directly from the content or from the database's meta-information itself, so the items it retrieves in the search are guaranteed to be relevant. In the end you are much more likely to find what you are looking for.

Scatter and Gather

Another way to look at this is as the 'scatter and gather' process. The first search term is the 'scattered' bait, thrown out to 'catch' the relevant terms and results. Therefore, the system not only retrieves the exact results, but also suggestions that appear further away from the original term. Thus, the gather process has begun. Every suggestion can also have its own 'scatter' and 'gather' follow-up.

Example: You are looking for 'Vermeer'. The search results that are retrieved are vast and general. They include construction companies, information on the artist and even farming equipment. An intelligent search system will make you aware of the different meanings of the term 'Vermeer'. In which context did you mean 'Vermeer'? If you are looking for the famous Dutch artist Vermeer who painted the "Girl with the Pearl Earring", then you put the suggested 'painter' term out as a 'gathering term' to enter into the world of the famous painter Johannes Vermeer. After this action, your result set will be more directed towards the painter Johannes Vermeer to further facilitate the search process.

In the scatter-gather process, you can use Vermeer to direct the search to 'artist', the 'Girl with the Pearl Earring' painting and so forth; continually retrieving results that are closer and closer to what you are looking for.

Professor Chanowski has a very particular view here. "The unpleasant truth is that intelligent search systems require fuzzy thinking in order to get exact relevant results. If you are not open to that, and when you stick to 'exactly' formulated search terms, you will never get to the most relevant results. The more structure you put in your query formulation, based on the set of knowledge that you have at the beginning of the search process, the more limited your results will be. This also means a higher chance for retrieving zero results. That is why we believe the public will never fully accept Boolean-based search systems or multiple query boxes, drop-down menus, linear specification lists, buttons and switches."

> This is why we believe a search system should always support the user's pre-existing knowledge while enriching his query formulation, even when the user knows exactly what he is looking for.

The above reflects why it is the intelligence of the search system that should add fuzzy, non-exact suggestions that will relate to the meaning of the search terms you use. If you search for 'bicycle', 'competition' and 'road-racing', and the system fails to alert you that 'cycling' is the better term to start with, you might loose the best information available on

Search and Accessibility

the history of the 'Tour the France' and the importance of Lance Armstrong in the recent Tour history.

"The interactive element of the search process is what gives you the most relevant answers, or even better questions. Therefore all the discussions of 'relevance ranking' are actually not that relevant. The relevance lies in the path that you, the user, takes. Then your search will result in a set of answers that are relevant to your actual desire for information. The serendipitous process of finding the best answer to your question is part of the entire search process; the scatter-gather process allows you to do this."

The statement above illustrates the importance of language and suggestions and the need for a single form of intelligence in the search system. This contrasts with old-style database searching, in which one must fill in according to strict categories (author, item, ISBN, or predefined classes such as history, culture, science, etc) or a set of predefined rules like Boolean search. This is the world reversed. Truly intelligent search systems themselves must be able to understand what you ask of them. And when they do not, they must still be able to come up with useful information that is relevant to your search.

> The serendipitous process of finding the best answer to your question is part of the entire search process; the scatter-gather process allows you to do this.

Professor Chanowski states that there are fundamental problems with any search and retrieval system based on the underlying database structure.

"This old idea comes from the period in time that we believed we needed to store all data in categories and boxes to be able to find it again later. This is still basically the way we store our documents on our personal computers. We quickly create categories like business, meetings, projects, customers, products, and private and public contacts. By the time you are finished, you cannot remember which boxes you have stored all this data in! There is an even bigger issue that is so familiar to the library realm. Most of this data can be placed into more than one categorical box. Database systems developed clever ways of working around this kind of issue, but the problem still remains. When you are looking in one category (author, title, subject etc.) you are actually overlooking the others. The typical library search system allows you to choose certain categories, but what you do not realize is that you are simultaneously eliminating others. The old systems work just as if you would be walking around in a car showroom, looking for a specific type of car, but explicitly NOT looking at any other model or type that is also very close to what you want."

The begin-user

A completely separate topic from Chanowski's is the need for one good search interface that couples a variety of sources. Chanowski calls this the dilemma of the so called 'end-'user. He claims that the term end-user matches perfectly with the old database paradigm. Chanowski states that the term end-user shouldn't have existed anyway. It should have been "begin-"user. Why are there different interfaces connecting to every different source? Many users are not interested in knowing that the information comes from a specific source, as long as it is a legitimate one. He wants to discover and see all the information there is on a given topic. Only later will the user care where and what source it came from. This may only be different for scientists and information professionals.

> The average user is definitely not interested in knowing that the information comes from a specific source, as long as it is a legitimate one.

"Consider the library. A search engine for the catalog is often built upon a database system with a web interface laid on over the OPAC. The fact is, on the Internet it is nearly the same. When we want to find general information about something we use an Internet search engine. In the library, we've got all the various search interfaces connecting to the data made available by the publishing houses and associated organizations. The library patron must log-in to search each individual database and use the corresponding search tool. It is impossible for the average library patron to learn to use all those different search tools, besides also being extremely inconvenient to do so." Even though some search tools allow the scope of the search to look outside the library's collection through a range of multiple external sources (federated search), they are in no way a solution or even a step closer to the search process described by Professor Chanowski. It is for these reasons that it is astonishing to see how few sources are actually used by library patrons.

> "It is impossible for the average library patron to learn to use all those different search tools, besides also being extremely inconvenient to do so."

Each integrated library system vendor offers a range of search solutions through their own portals. It is more a 'scraping together' of search methodologies. First there is the OPAC search interface for the catalog. Then there are other interfaces to specific collections. And finally within the portals there is often another sub-interface to the 'federated search' sources. Sometimes a meta-search technology integrates these together, but this again means a new search structure is necessary for the user. Logically, it follows that the user is bombarded with more things they do not understand. It can be chaos. You can count up seven different sources with just as many search systems. How can this possibly be attractive to the masses?

Instead, the library should look to technologies that can supply an intelligent method to integrate all the sources at once. This means combining its own catalog, a set of websites, the databases of partner institutions, local cultural associations and online vendors, all together in an intelligent collective.

Professor Chanowski looks at modern, intelligent search technologies as systems that handle all sources of information as if they were placed in a liquid environment. They should be able to freely move around within the domain of content: like fish in an aquarium. The fish represent all the sources and items of information. The boundaries of the aquarium, the glass panes, are set by the owner (the library in this case). The owner defines the boundaries, how much, large, tall, the volume, the quality and the quantity of the fish. When a user poses a question, it is like baiting the fish. The users can feed from any angle, perspective, or type of bait. Those fish that are very hungry, or very large with a bit of an appetite, should be able to move unhindered towards the food. Those hungriest fish will get to the food first, other fish will arrive a bit later, and fish who have no appetite for that particular bait will stay where they are. Then maybe on the next feeding, from a bit of a different angle or with a slightly different rod and reel, the group of attracted fish slightly changes; again some go, while others appear. All of the fish share a common behaviour: they are free to move back and forth, in different co-occurrences and through different groups. This will happen as long as there are fish in the aquarium that continue to go after the bait.

Professor Chanowski, like R.S. Ranganathan, sees the serendipitous finding of information completely vital to the search process. "We have all looked for a specific book and in the process discovered one we absolutely needed next to it or even on the opposite shelf," stated Ranganathan. He also pointed out that most patrons have no idea about some of the 'hidden' resources that are available in the library collections. Professor Chanowski says this: "I see the library, or the virtual library to be a liquid environment. For any patron who enters, the whole library is re-ranked and reorganized towards his question. After his next question the same will happen again. The library itself should behave like a huge fluid environment towards each individual and each individual question. Any library that structures itself in a rigid way and only provides its patrons access to this rigid structure and does not offer the best possible means to browsing and linking is being neglectful.

Most libraries fail to provide an environment where serendipity can freely occur."

Professor Chanowski, like R.S. Ranganathan, sees the serendipitous finding of information completely vital to the search process.

Again it is this kind of neglect that could also lead us to the path from in the introduction, of 2012 and a world without public libraries. This world would only leave room for mediocre sources and information because it would lack the space for the serendipitous finding.

Some say that Socrates repeatedly stated, "I only know that I do not know." One could say that this phrase is a healthy reminder of our limitations concerning wisdom. And it is still valid; the universe is so wide, life is so complex that, no matter how much we study it, unsolved mysteries will always remain. New knowledge will quickly replace old knowledge. There is no absolute knowledge. In The Republic (Plato, the cave) Socrates describes the 'divided line', a continuum from ignorance (including the visible world) to knowledge (the intelligible world) with the Good (the true, ideal knowledge) on top of it all. Something which we can pursue but never will reach completely. In his words, "Truth lies beneath the shadows of existence and it is the job of the philosopher to show the rest how little they know." How did Socrates do that? He did it by asking questions, by introducing the dialogue to his students, the pursuers of knowledge. He believed that the highest form of human excellence was the process to question oneself and others. This offers a universe of questions to help you to answer your question. The dialogue has been and still is one of the most important assets in philosophy and ultimately, in the sciences. Hypothesis leads to thesis, which in turn can be questioned, or be falsified.

The eminent Sir Karl Popper, one of the most influential philosophers of science of the 20th century, has asserted that no empirical hypothesis, proposition, or theory can be considered scientific if it does not admit the possibility of a contrary case, a counter-question, so to say. Falsifiable does not mean false. For a proposition to be falsifiable, it must be possible, at least in principle, to make an observation that would show the proposition failing to be a tautology (which is always 'true'), even if that observation is not made.

The proposition "All swans are white" would be falsified by observing a black swan, which would in turn depend on there being a black swan somewhere in existence (which of course there are). A falsifiable proposition or theory must define in some way what is, or will be, forbidden by that proposition or theory. For example, in this case the existence of a black swan is forbidden by the proposition in question. The possibility of observing a black swan as a counterexample to the general proposition is sufficient to qualify the proposition as falsifiable.

Now let's get back to the current issue, intelligent library search systems. The dialogue keeps the quest for knowledge alive, thanks to Socrates' passion for knowledge. The dialogue is the path that a lover of wisdom must take in pursuing it. An intelligent search system should allow us to execute our search process accordingly: through dialog.

Identity versus reality

We recently went to a conference in San Antonio. One evening during our visit, we spoke to a friend of ours, Dianne Coan, from our partner company – The Library Corporation. Blabbering in our jet-lag about the future of public libraries, we talked about the 'stuffy image' the library had and which seemed impossible to break. Dianne told us an entertaining story about a visitor she had over at her home.

The Free Book Store

"My visitor was a friend of a friend, and when I returned home from volunteering at our local library, this person asked where I had been. I explained that there was this totally innovative place called the 'Free Book Store'. Her eyes got big and she wanted to know more. At the free book store anybody can come in and essentially borrow any of the books, CD's and movies that they owned for about 3 weeks. If you bring it back late, there may be a really small fee, but nothing compared to heading to a retail store and buying all the stuff you wanted. Furthermore there's even free wireless Internet access at this place. I also explained that the free book store had a database or catalog of all the materials in its system. You can access this

from anywhere via the web and even reserve the items you want to pick up on your next visit. You can get services like home-work help, as well as assistance from people who help you find stuff you are looking for and offer some research assistance if you run into trouble."

The visitor listening to Dianne was totally enthralled. She told Dianne she thought the concept was fantastic: "A free book-store, how revolutionary. Gosh, I wish I had one of these in my neighborhood," said the woman. Holding back from rolling her eyes, Dianne finally gave in and stated bluntly, "um, hello, I'm talking about the public library." The woman, probably slightly embarrassed replied, "Oh? Oh." She reacted as if she were dis-appointed, actually.

The moral here is that the library, the word 'library' has a stigma to it. That stigma is what keeps the public from running to it in droves to check out materials and make use of all the great and FREE services it offers. The same stigma is what makes a library website the last place people will go to look for information. They simply don't realize that libraries offer their entire catalogs and more – all online, from any-where, inside or outside of the physical library. This is all more evidence that it is the image of the public library in society that should change in order to increase interest. If a simple thing like calling the library 'the free bookstore' makes people interested, then so be it. We live in a consumer-based society and we will have to tailor the public library to fit into that society rather than resist it. Making the library even more attractive to the public –by changing the identity- will in no way lessen the quality of the information that is held within its walls.

Today any identity is largely defined by web identity. This is cer-tainly true for companies and people alike.

A good example of this change is your average 15 year old student. Ten years ago the social life and identity of such a student was derived from experiences in the class and during recess on the school grounds.

Back then, when you asked the student how many peers he knew by name, he would probably give you an answer between 50 and 100. The high-point from their social life was found during recess where one had the best chances of meeting and getting to know other students. These were one-on-one contacts that formed, one at a time into social groupings. A 'busy' period during recess would entail speaking with 12 other people!

Today this situation has completely changed. The social life at school is still very important but the high-point of social life plays out after school, via blogs, instant messaging, websites, homepages, web-cams, email, mobile phones (with cameras), text-messaging, multiplay-er web games and online communities. When you now ask the average student how many peers he knows by name, the answer will easily be 250. These relations are one-on-one, one-to-many, and now thanks to instant messaging and online communities, many-to-many. During these online hours our student communicates with up to 50 people at once while using 3 or 4 different types of communication. And during this socializing, the image, or way we identify that person is greatly built up by their blogs, the colors and images they choose on their per-sonal website, their instant messaging handle, their responsiveness and the online communities in which they participate.

Web identity

Successful companies that in fact have nothing to do with the web have learned that access to their products and services actually depends on the web. The new rule seems to be that only when there is unin-hibited online access to your products and services can a company be successful. The same goes for the company's identity. Successful com-panies often have easy web accessibility and an attractive web identity.

This is all exactly the same for the library. We believe the future and success of the public library is heavily dependent on a positive web identity. The representation of the library via the web, the library's web identity, is now, and will increasingly be, a key asset.

The web identity of the library should be clear both to itself and its users. If the library is the information guide, then the website should reflect that. If the aggregation of local sources and integration of the catalog search is a key element of the library's mission, then the website should reflect that. If the library is the responsible source for information that pertains to an individual community, then its website should reflect that. If the local library creates specific collections composed of expertise on something related to that local area, then the website should reflect this expertise.

We believe that the library homepage should be easily identifiable by the library's key asset, namely the collection (regional, local, specialized). The collection should be only a click away from the homepage, or from any other webpage in the site. We even feel that the library's homepage should directly represent what is in the collection. What this all comes down to is that we see that the search box connects the user to the entire aggregated collection and it should prominently appear on every page. It's actually just that simple.

> We believe the future and success of the public library
> is heavily dependent on a positive web identity. The
> representation of the library via the web, the library's web
> identity, will be a key asset.

Here is a quick aside to explain what we mean. For Google, their identity and main asset is searching the web. www.google.com leads you directly to a totally uncluttered website with a search box that accesses most sites in the World Wide Web. The Google website is the Google identity. Google identity is… search. So, the Google website is a search box. No tabs, no options, no questions asked, no categories, no pull downs, no clicks needed to get to it. Their main asset is search and we directly identify the Google homepage with searching. Google is a vast and complex organization of thousands of employees performing hundreds of services and activities. If you think about what Google actually does, their website could have looked tremendously different!

Now let's have a look at a typical public library website from an 'image' point of view. What does it actually say? What is the identity? You can probably find out the library's opening hours, local news, new books, their vision, mission statement and the local weather. You will often find a list of tabs with items such as 'About the Library', 'Branches', 'Policies', 'Upcoming Events', 'News', 'eSources' (Databases and more), 'OPAC', 'Collections and Services', 'Contact Us', 'Job openings', and 'FAQs'. But if we agree on the idea that the main asset is the library's collection, is it really that easy to get in touch with it and begin a search through the collection? The typical library homepage contributes to the blurry image that the library is a complex organization that offers many options, activities, services, visions and methodologies. It relates to the institute, the organization. Is this really what the visitor of a library website should be looking for? Aren't most of us just trying to find a book or a piece of information?

It's not just the OPAC

If we all agree that the collection is the library's main asset, then we should identify what hinders public access to that collection. We know all the stories, complaints and even a song about how bad the OPAC is. But we think the OPAC certainly isn't the only factor upon which blame should be placed. We will now identify some of these other factors which, from our perspective, could pose issues for the library.

1. Click, click, click

Fist of all, on a typical library website, you need to figure out were you can access the library collection. We found that on 90% of the library homepages we viewed, the user needs to make at least two or three more clicks to get to any search environment that opens a source. From this perspective, the library web identity is more like that of a poorly organized corporate website with information on its pages that is introspective, vague and often, useless. A vision is a great thing for a library to have, but can you tell me how many patrons will access the site, with the burning question, "what's my library's mission, I wonder?" No, we feel the local patron accessing the library's site is searching for specific information and wants to enter a search query, hit enter and go!

2. Options, options, options

Secondly, once you get to the box to enter a search term, the library's true identity is often hidden by their offer of databases and search methodologies. What kind of search do you want? Classic search, Advanced search, Boolean search? And where do you want to search? In the "OPAC", eSources, or search the website? Is there a world-wide standard that defines what classic and advanced are? Did I ever learn what on earth a Boolean search is in school, and if so, do I remember? Would I really want to search an "OPAC"? Do I know what an OPAC is? The end result here is that the library identity on search and accessibility becomes that of an institution that offers all kinds of databases and search methodologies. We think for most people this is a scary place.

3. Doesn't really work

Thirdly, the library's web identity with search is completely misleading in many cases. We found public library websites with search boxes on the homepage that lead to search results of the public library's site itself, and sometimes connected to one or two well-intentioned databases. Library identity on search and accessibility simply becomes that of an organization that offers search that doesn't really work. First impressions will tell all. We all know today's Internet users only try once or twice. After that, the identity will become "doesn't work". Would you blame a patron for avoiding the site if every time they attempted to search a term in the query box they are confronted with results 'about the library'?

4. Dusty old DOS

Fourth: identity blur has to do with the search technology that is used. In many public library websites, after you have found the web-page that leads you to the catalog search, you are confronted with a particular search technology from the catalog management system; in many cases, a completely outdated ugly DOS-looking kind of screen, with fields, boxes and pull down menus. Suddenly the library identity on search and accessibility of the collection becomes one of outdated software that NOBODY is using anymore or likely wants to use; a col-lection of dusty old books, using dusty old technology.

5. http://www.parhump.gov.us.org/County/Departments/librar-ies/main

Fifth: Have you ever thought about the library website URL? You presume that the URL for the Parhump Public Library website would be "http://www.parhumppubliclibrary.org' or 'http://www.ppl.org'. However, it turns out, it's actually 'http://www.parhump.gov.us.org/County/Departments/libraries/main', or something crazy like that. The simple fact of having an over-complicated URL will keep many people from using the library's website.

6. There is no library

When you try to search for anything in a search engine you never seem to get the library as a result. You also never see items from within the library that relate to your search engine query as a result. Have you ever wondered why most subject searches in a search engine give you Wikipedia entries as the first or second result? While not showing the local public library URL? The library web identity for most people who are searching on the web is: there is no library.

7. Speed

Most web search engines show you phrases like "We found 235,647 results for you in 0.26 seconds!" People are getting used to this. Compare this with a typical library web search: "Oh man, this is slow".

8. The middle man

Then finally, the library's true identity is blurred by their offering of an array of different database collections to search. This is like being confronted with the reaction, "Oh, you want to know something about cultural history? Well, why not try to have a look in Publisher Collection one, Publisher Collection two, Publisher Collection three, Publisher Collection four, and so forth. Oh, and by the way, each collection will force you to use its own specific way of searching." In this last example, the library identity is that of an institution that offers all kinds of collections with names that do not put you any closer to answering your original question. Some libraries offer specific search entrances to (parts of) the external collections (federated search), but in practice those technologies just represent another additional access-point to information. Your library now has the identity of 'the middle man'. He may get you in touch with a place he once heard might have had something you're looking for.

The library's web identity should be as clear as the sign on the front door of the physical building, welcoming the patron into the collection. It is the collection that the public identifies the library with, and the library should therefore promote its collection far and wide. Today's podium: the web. One way to promote the library's identity through its collection is by actually removing technical branding; de-emphasize differences in sources and simplifying what a user sees when he goes to a library homepage. We believe that most users would want to visit a library website to find information in the collection, the same users who are using the Internet search engines to find information from web pages. If that is the simple goal, then the interface they see should first and foremost help the user to reach that goal. Anything else provided beyond the name of the library and a query box should only be there if it is useful to the user. We are convinced that the user is not primarily interested in the name of the ILS, the search platform, the name of the eSource or the name of the OPAC their library offers. Most patrons will not even know what an OPAC is. They should instead see the library name and a simple query box allowing all those underlying intelligent search technologies and processes to do the work and get to the collection without interference. The look and feel of the website may of course reflect the physical library's and its community's identity.

> One way to promote the library's identity through its collection is by actually removing technical branding; de-emphasize differences in sources and simplifying what a user sees when he goes to a library homepage.

The library's identity and the library's web identity must be one in the same. Like the consumer websites that provide products and services, the library should emulate them in the same manner. The physical library might be meticulously organized, the web access should require no pre-knowledge or methodology whatsoever, adding up to the library's web identity of collection openness and accessibility. The library has to see its web identity as the window into the collection and not as a massive filing cabinet into which any and all items are shoved.

All of this talk of simplifying the library website may sound as if we are suggesting assimilating all libraries into one box. On the contrary, because every library's collection becomes the way in which they are identified, there will only be even more differentiation between public libraries. Each individual library is founded on the needs of its own community. Every community in the world has its own identifying factors. And this identity is what the library represents. The information that is either unique or the most useful to every community is what their own library must promote at the highest level.

This is how the public will realize the value of its own library and seek out the quality information the library holds directly. This is a way to get the people back into the library.

Mind games

Although many libraries are managed like companies, it seems as if their marketing and communications activities do not follow the same model. The library does not seem to realize what an important ingredient marketing is in running a business. Even though a company offers a non web-related product or service, the identity of the whole enterprise could still largely be colored by its web presence. This may be because the organization has chosen to make the web the podium for product positioning. It can also be that the company uses the web as a means to build a stronger identity directed at a web-minded public.

In comparison with a large portion of the business world, the library has a fantastic opportunity. What is different from most companies is that the library has a direct connection with the use of the web, both in operations and for its patrons. The thinking of library patrons (both public and academic) and their need for information is broad.

The web already plays a special role in the way library business is done. As with business, the library needs to build up its web identity, and it doesn't even need to start from scratch to do so. The elements to realize a strong, established web presence are all there but it is up to the library to use those elements to claim its role in the patrons' minds. How exactly do we mean this, precisely? Here is our ambition:

> *When any child, student, adult, elderly person or simply, any citizen, should need any piece of information, the image of the library homepage should pop up into his mind first. The library in the role of the most trustworthy guide in the information landscape is able to direct and re-direct any citizen to the information he needs inside or outside the library collection.*

Identity Versus Reality

Most importantly the library website lives up to and exceeds the promise to fulfil this role in its community. By continually getting this right, the citizen will always come back.

The library web identity should portray this.

Let us look at business examples in practice. In an effort to stay 'close to home', we'll look specifically at the site of Royal Dutch Airlines (KLM). When we go to www.klm.com we are directly faced with a search and booking menu to buy plane tickets. There is no information on how ticketing works, about the various types of tickets available, categories, ticket classes, the fleet of planes which KLM flies, or the layout of various airports. Thus the website is marketing their core proposition: getting you from point A to B. During the booking process, I am offered choices that are relevant –at that particular moment-, and after I've completed my online booking transaction, I may receive more information on KLM's partners, or a new service offered by KLM. But the primary goal of booking a ticket is immediately achievable from the get-go. The point here is that only the most relevant information for both the company's goal (selling tickets) and the consumer's goal (getting from A to B) is given at the first step. All information that is not directly related to these goals is placed elsewhere.

The website is marketing their core proposition: getting you from point A to B.

At the time this is being written, Air France-KLM, created through a 2004 merger, together form one of the largest and most profitable airline networks in the world. This alliance also has one of the most highly rated levels of customer satisfaction with a loyal customer base.

Thus what KLM has achieved is that anytime a Dutch consumer wants to get from point A to B he will think of the KLM website first and automatically go to it. He knows exactly how to find the website and he is secure that he will be able to book his tickets online within one or two clicks. Most importantly, the KLM website lives up to and exceeds the promise to fulfil the customer's needs. By continually getting this right the consumer will always come back.

Another example is in the case of Apple. iPod mp3 players have taken the world by storm. They make up the majority of all mp3 players sold in the world, and they are the highest selling product from Apple. Let's presume that I have decided I want to buy a new mp3 player. I first think of the iPod and know I have to search on the Apple website. Despite the fact that Apple is a large complex technology corporation with services and sales points worldwide, when I go to the Apple homepage I am faced right away with an attractive and simple product overview. The full iPod is just one click away.

What Apple has achieved is that anytime a worldwide customer wants to know something about the iPod he thinks of the Apple website first and automatically goes to it. He knows exactly how to find the Apple website and he is secure that he will encounter the world of iPods and all there is to know about them. Most importantly, the Apple website lives up to and exceeds the promise to fulfill the customer's needs. By continually getting this right, the prospective iPod customers will remain loyal to the Apple web identity and will take the effort to order an iPod online, or go to a store to purchase one.

How easy is it to get it wrong? In Europe, up until two years ago, Nokia was the hottest mobile phone anyone could get. Nokia offered the best combination of features, design and image. For reasons we are unsure of, the popularity and sales of Nokia products has dropped off. We are not saying this is directly due to the Nokia corporate website but today it is difficult to locate information about their products on their site.

We begin with the desire to find information on the latest popular model, the Nokia 5200. Sitting in Amsterdam as we write this, we go to the www.nokia.com website. First we are confronted with choosing one of three buttons in order to proceed; Business Solutions, Corporate Information, or Phones and More. We click on Phones and More

Identity Versus Reality

and then we are faced with selecting a worldwide region. We choose Europe and then we must choose our country. The Netherlands is not on the list of choices, in fact, the list stops at the letter 'L'. So we decide to choose our neighbor country, Belgium. A new screen opens and we must now choose between three languages, English, French or Dutch. We choose Dutch. Finally we are on the Nokia Benelux homepage which represents the Netherlands, Belgium and Luxembourg. On the homepage we find the option 'Look for a mobile phone' with subcategories: 20 Latest, Entire Collection, Compare Phones, Camera Phones, Nseries and N-Gage. Luckily on the same page there is a special feature on three different models, and one of them is the 5200. We click on it, and a new browser window opens! Choose your language... We choose Dutch. After 15 seconds the site loads and a Flash animation starts running.

First we are confronted with choosing one of three buttons in order to proceed; Business Solutions, Corporate Information, or Phones and More.

The point is: What is the identity of Nokia that remains in our minds? We now relate Nokia's web identity to multiple choice questionnaires, irrelevant options, unknown categories, and wasting time. Through this experience it is now difficult for us to differentiate between the Nokia web identity and Nokia's products.

It will be clear that we foresee the web identity of the library becoming comparable to the examples we gave of KLM and Apple.

When any child, student, adult, elderly person or simply, any citizen, should need any piece of information, he should think of his local public library website first.

Like KLM and Apple the library should be the website that people go to when they want to search for information. People should be able to easily find the library website and perform a search right away, from entry, on the entire collection.

The library in the role of the most trustworthy guide in the information landscape is able to direct and redirect any citizen to the information he needs inside or outside the library collection.

People should be reassured that the information the library offers through the website represents the actual physical collection as well as connects to relevant verified sources outside the library.

Most importantly the library website lives up to and exceeds the promise to fulfil this role to its community.

By continually getting this right the citizen will always come back.

Being there

Now here's another identity versus reality issue. It is the public perception of the Internet search engines, and what they actually are.

The use of technology by the library to 'compete' with broad Internet searches reaches far and wide. But even if the content in the library was just as easily reached by all who choose to use it there shouldn't be a competition with Internet searching. The best information can only be found through a multitude of means and sources. The Internet search has a role here. It is the library's responsibility to create and offer an environment that can do this all at once in order to remain relevant and efficient to the user. The library's web identity will influence how people will perceive this relevance.

One of the reasons the library must now concentrate on developing its web identity is that without it, the biggest fear of the library world will come true. The Internet will take over the role of the library as the only source people will go to for information. A misconception that has arisen through the emergence of search engines is the perception that all information that exists can be found on the Internet. The misconception goes even further to convey that this information is all

Identity Versus Reality

true and factual. There is a presumption given to search engines that the most popular search result is always placed on top of the list. You hear the stories about younger students making statements similar to, "It's true, because I 'Googled' it." They will use a search engine to find information for their school work, and once they've viewed the first one or two results, they feel the search is over. These actions cater to the impressions that Internet search engines actually own all the information.

Search engines were never created to replace libraries. Internet search engine companies themselves do make clear that they have no ambition whatsoever to claim this role. It will be the user in the end, who will determine which one will be the information guide for them.

They are positioning themselves as one of many 'messengers' of information which can be found on the Internet. For this reason search engines put explanations on their homepages that they cannot be held responsible for what can be found with their search technology. Despite the disclaimers, the public perception that something which has been found with the search engine is 'the truth' and even belongs to the search engine company will continue to exist.

> The best information can only be found through a
> multitude of means and sources.

Given the idea the Internet search engines never had the intention to take the library's role the story from the novel and film by Jerzy Kozinsky 'Being There' about Chance the gardener comes to mind.

Chance grows up in the townhouse of a wealthy man in Washington D.C. where he is totally deprived of the outside world and almost deprived of social contacts, except for some limited interaction with the maid. He gets his cultural and social education entirely from the TV's of his master. So, he grows up staying in the house and tending the garden until the old man dies. By now a middle-aged man, he is forced to leave the place and has to survive the 'real' world. Dressed in old-fashioned clothes he roams the streets of Washington until a car accident puts him in contact with a powerful businessman and his wife who believe that he is a bankrupt businessman. Asked for his name while offered a strong drink, he coughs "Chance the gardener" which is interpreted as 'Chauncy Gardiner'. The couple befriends him and is impressed by his simplistic language, which they interpret as profound wisdom.

The businessman is also an advisor of the President of the U.S. Chance 'knows' the president from TV and when they meet he speaks of "the garden that changes with the seasons", which the President sees as a philosophical quote on politics and economy and uses it in a TV speech. The speech is acclaimed and with every next quote Chance's stardom rises, and rises quickly, even though nobody knows who he is and where he came from.

The businessman becomes very ill and eventually dies. Before his death he encourages his wife to become close with Chance. At the funeral, the President's obituary for his friend is amply filled with Chance's quotes and there are murmurs in the audience that 'Chauncy Gardiner' might be the next candidate for Presidency. But does Chance care?

Just like it was never Chance's intention to become President, it was never the intention of Internet search engines to replace the library. Internet search engine's sources are not specified and the algorithms that are used to calculate the ranking are protected as the best kept secrets of all time. The masses tend to trust the oracle. "With every next quote Chance's star rises, and rises quickly, even though nobody knows who he is and where he came from." We shouldn't allow the Internet search engine to 'run for president'. We believe it is the natural role of the library to reconfirm and to regain its classic identity of being the trustworthy guide in the information landscape.

Golden opportunities

No matter what industry you look at, golden opportunities do not occur easily or frequently. It is because of this all too important fact that the current opportunity for the library needs to be recognized and action must be taken. Getting people back to the library by improving its web identity represents the golden opportunity the public library has today. The quality advantage is obvious. Web technologies are available. And there are so many ways to use the good part of the Internet and incorporate it in the quality library offering.

The library market has remained relatively calm in recent years. There have been, of course, important technological breakthroughs, but the processes have not really changed.

The market is about to change, however. The web based communication and interaction world is not quiet, but rather it is a world of incredible development with incredible momentum. While the library can assume a period of calm for the foreseeable future in its vision and it can believe it holds some sort of competitive advantages over other information sources, the developments in the past 3-5 years and those that are coming in the next several years will certainly turn that vision upside down.

> Getting people back to the library by improving its web identity represents the golden opportunity the public library has today.

In order to get patrons back into the library, the library needs to reinvent its web identity, its image on the web, not itself. The library has been on an evolutionary path, slowly reclaiming its role as the information guide, as it was historically. We believe the benefits of taking the technology that had robbed the library of its role and applying them to improving the free access to quality information will be immeasurable. The library now can simply embrace all the modern services and technologies that allow them to provide better access to their main asset over the Web. Technology that almost took the library's power away is now giving it back. It is the function of change; we have crossed the line. Today the pain that comes from not changing is way beyond the pain of adopting new, intelligent web-based search technologies to open up the catalog and, in the next step, the entire collection.

Around 1800, the brothers Jacob Ludwig Carl Grimm and Wilhelm Karl Grimm traveled widely through Germany and adjacent countries, performing field research for their linguistic work, which involved trying to find patterns in how the vowels and consonants which made up specific words changed over time. To determine these patterns, they needed to hear many different examples of authentic speech by various speakers of different ages and in different regions. They eventually discovered that one of the easiest ways to convince older local residents to give them lengthy examples of their natural speech was to ask the residents to tell their favorite stories to the brothers. As the brothers recorded the style of speech of the speaker for their research, they also recorded the various stories that they were told, and eventually published them in 1817. The stories became immensely popular in Europe, and were widely reprinted. Ironically, the brothers are now most widely known for these collections of stories, which were essentially an unexpected by-product of the linguistic research, which was their primary goal.

One of their better known stories is about the youngest daughter of a king. She was a lover of objects made of gold. Her favorite toy in the world was a golden ball. On hot days, she liked to sit beside a well in the cool forest, tossing the ball in the air. One day, it slipped from her fingers and plunged into the well, which was so deep that the princess could not see the bottom. "Poor me! I'll never find it!" the princess cried.

Suddenly a frog stuck his head out of the water and asked what she was lamenting about.

Identity Versus Reality

"Oh, you horrid frog," she said, "what can you do to help me? My golden ball has fallen into the well." She wasn't even surprised that he could talk…

But the frog said, "If you will take me home as your companion, and I shall sit near you and eat from your plate and if you will love me, I will bring back your ball."

"Oh well", she said, "I promise."

The frog plunged under the water, retrieved her ball, and threw it onto land. The king's daughter grabbed it and ran away, ignoring the frog's calls to take him with her. Back in the castle she had just sat down for dinner when she heard something coming up the staircase, splashing and soon there was a knock on the door, and a voice cried "King's daughter, open up for me!" She ran to open the door; but seeing that it was the frog, slammed it again and returned to the table. "Out there is this horrid frog, she said to the king, who fetched my golden ball out of the water for me. I promised him that he should be my companion, now he is outside and wants to come in." And she started crying.

> "If you will take me home as your companion and I shall sit near you and eat from your plate and if you will love me, I will bring back your ball."

"You have made a promise and you have to keep your promise", he answered. She opened the door for the frog, and he followed her to the dining table. And he said to her, "Put me next to you at the table, I want to eat with you." She looked at him with disgust and refused until the king ordered her again to make it happen. So the frog sat at her side and when he had eaten enough, he said to her, "Take me to your bed, I want to sleep beside you."

The thought of sharing her room with the cold damp frog upset the princess and she began to cry again. But the king said, "Be on your way. It's not right to turn your back on someone who helped you when you were in trouble".

"Alright, father," said the princess reluctantly, and she carefully picked up the frog with two fingers, shuddering. When she got to her room, she quickly put the frog down in the corner farthest from her bed. But soon she heard the frog plop down beside her. "I'm tired, too," said the frog. "Lift me into bed, or I'll tell your father." So the princess tucked the frog into bed, with his little green head resting on a fluffy pillow.

But when she got back into her bed herself, she was surprised to hear the frog sobbing quietly. "What's the matter now, little frog?" she asked. "All I ever wanted was a friend," the frog replied. "But it's clear you don't like me at all! I might as well go back to the cold well." At this, the princess started to feel very badly indeed. And she made a decision and she bowed over to the small green creature. "I'll be your friend," she said, and this time she meant it. Then the princess gave him a kiss goodnight on his small green cheek.

And instantly, the frog was transformed into a very handsome young prince. The princess could not have been more surprised or pleased. Of course the prince and princess married a few years later and lived happily ever after.

Identity versus Reality. We'd opt for a strong focus on a clear and unmistakable web identity. The golden ball is in the hands of the library now. Let's become true friends with the Internet and Chance the gardener. For the public library realm, the frog years are behind us now.

Library Vendor Challenges

Europa was the daughter of Agenor, the Phoenician king of Tyre (today a town in Lebanon). One early morning she was walking towards the beach with her companions, all young women of her age. It was a beautiful day and they went off to gather flowers from the meadows by the sea where cattle were grazing. The mighty Zeus noticed the group and having an insatiable interest in human females, he was more than charmed by Europa, by far the prettiest of all. So he lowered himself and took the shape of a snow white bull and he appeared among the cattle. Europa noticed him, first because of his impressive size and then for his beautiful fur and his long horns, shimmering like pearls. But she was cautious. So he slowly moved closer, carrying flowers in his mouth, and offered them to her. Looking in his friendly eyes, her initial caution vanished quickly and she followed him to the sandy beach and touched him carefully. He did not move and allowed her to decorate his head with the fresh flowers and she praised him for his gentleness. Now that Europa trusted him, he laid down as if to invite her to climb on his back, which she did.

When she sat on his back he got up carefully and walked to the shore with her and then slowly entered the sea. Then, unexpectedly, he started to swim faster and faster and Europa had to hold on firmly, her clothes fluttering in the breeze. She became afraid and started questioning her decision and action and then, when she looked back, she was absolutely terrified. The shore had become small in the distance. Even worse, the wind had risen and the waves were becoming higher. The bull was accelerating even more and she started to cry in despair. And when she thought things could not become worse Nereids riding on dolphins came out of the waves. Nereids, daughters of Nereus and Doris, always friendly and helpful towards sailors fighting storms, started to hail the bull and she realized that she had been deceived and taken away by a divinity. And when Zeus finally revealed his true character to her she was screaming with fear and pleaded with him to pity her. But he ignored her panic and her tears and made for the shores of the island of Crete to do as he pleased.

> Now that Europa trusted him, he laid down as if to invite
> her to climb on his back, which she did.

It is not that difficult for clients of older, large integrated software vendors to identify with Europa. Companies that offer such integrated software, often take their customers on a carousel ride, providing them with all they need and more. However, as time progresses, the carousel spins ever faster and the customers can no longer seem to get off. And like Europa versus Zeus, they have become part of such a large system that their voices become small and unheard. In reality, the setting and the final outcome of the vendor-customer relationship is not as dramatic as Europa's story, but it is true that most of the major software players in the ILS (Integrated Library Systems) vendor market are older, established companies. Many of them were founded years ago and have since changed ownership or have gone through mergers multiple times. Their software products are application-based with high and huge demands that carry technical constraints and burdening installations. Typically, these products all have yearly support agreements, with contracts for durations from 3 to 5 years, and an impressive range of components, modules and functionalities.

The library vendors steered most of their developments towards the improvement of the library's internal processes, building bridges between all the different systems, and keeping the oldest systems alive through adaptations in order to stay in pace with the technology frontrunners, operating systems and software platform providers from outside the library market. It is only more recently actually, that a number of established ILS vendors actually begun to acknowledge their customers' web front-end demands. Most vendors tend to pay more attention to their competition, rather than really looking after their own customers' needs. They are busy analyzing each other's products and speculating as to what features will be offered in the future. Many vendors seem to market their products and position themselves by means of 'me too' functionality. With continuous copying and not much innovation, in our opinion there is only modest attention given to the actual needs of the customers.

At the same time, outside the library software realm, many things have happened and still are happening at an exhausting pace. No longer are we just talking about Google here, or Amazon; YouTube or wild market successes like the iPod. There are more subtle movements and processes going on in the software industry that are hitting the application-based companies in the heart of their existence. It's an afront aimed right at their 'reason for being': making money with the sale of software licences. The new, subtle IT movement that is going on has embraced a completely new paradigm. An important change has occured with the distinction between, and separation of, the back-end, transaction and storage applications involved in the product proposition from the front-end, directed at the web-presence emphasizing simple user-access and interactions. We envision a fully new IT software industry that is about to appear and take over the reigns of the application based software establishment.

> Many vendors seem to market their products and position themselves by means of 'me too' functionality.

We will illustrate the process that is taking place - up until today apparently unnoticed by the library industry - through an interesting real life example. It perfectly illustrates the subtle movement, with the enormous impact, which we tried to describe above.

The new software paradigm

It was only a very short period of time ago that almost all CRM (Customer Relation Management) and PM (Project Management) application software vendors were virtually the same. Both CRM and PM markets had become stalled environments; completely halted, full stop. They all had the exact same functionality, and there were no real standouts left. The products were rigidly defined, their feature lists were endless, pricing models were identical, and distribution models were fixed. The market was completely saturated and the number of vendors was way too high. It was almost impossible to differentiate. The main differentiation became the level of service an organization offered.

Recently a couple of CRM and PM companies went in a completely new direction. They took a careful look at what was going on, drew their conclusions and decided that it was time for a change; a big, and fundamental change. The Internet provided the platform for new visions and executions in product development, software distribution and the way people were working together.

What they concluded was the following.

Most established software companies in the CRM and PM realm are highly self-obsessed. Their internal organization, their product vision, functionality and their competition all reflect this. They are busy re-engineering their own products, improving their competitor's product functionality and spending huge amounts of money on analyzing and guessing what their competitor future features will be. The CRM and PM realm is a densely populated one; there are (too) many vendors and product versions that basically all do the same thing. With continuous copying and hardly any innovation left, there is little attention given to what the customers actually want. The products become filled with features customers never use, yet they all pay for them.

The next thing these new pioneers concluded was that most CRM and PM software companies had become funded by capital investment companies. These companies look at ROI (return on investment) and cash performance. At the end of the day It is questionable how beneficial this is to the end-user. The software vendor that is ROI-motivated tends not to focus on what is best for the customers, but more likely thinks in terms of cost-efficiency. The first areas cut in this case are often new product development & product innovation (which are usually the most expensive parts to the software development process) and the management focus is placed on keeping the wheels turning. The vendors become driven by the bottom line and no longer provide innovative products targeted at their customers interests.

> The software vendor that is ROI-motivated tends not to focus on what is best for the customers, but more likely thinks in terms of cost-efficiency.

Another very important observation the pioneers made was that most CRM and PM software companies did all of this at their own cost; they are closed, proprietary-focused with hardly any cost and technology sharing between them. Every major vendor tried to compete on the same level. In this manner, they all develop their unique integrated proprietary based systems and solutions. Everything is developed in-house completely at the individual company's expense. The processes, products, systems and technologies that go into them are based on individual development. Their customers not only paid for this in the end, but never really received anything new. Instead of focusing on what is best for the users, most CRM and PM vendors ended up building large expensive clones of each others products.

There was another interesting observation they made. Most software vendors had over-complicated their products to attempt to keep their most demanding customers happy. The actual software license, support and implementation fees are related to this complexity. They end up with the typical and very unpopular 80/20 rule. 80% of the customers are paying for complexity they hardly need or use themselves.

Breakthrough

The CRM and PM innovators placed their observations and conclusions on top of the speedy evolution that was going on in the Internet. They made a remarkable breakthrough in software development and building software businesses. They decided to redirect their development efforts to that 20% portion of really critical functionality. At the same time they freed the customer from the burden of software ownership, installation, customization, upgrading and updating policies. The concept of web-based services was born. Software functionality in a new form of web based services, reduced to its basic functional set while keeping the user completely satisfied (not to be confused with over-simplified marketing-driven 'lite' versions). It is smarter, faster, easier and much cheaper to create and maintain. It is a new direct way to build and bring software functionality to the user. Where traditional software license models and ASP (application service provider) solutions are characterized by the transfer of user license, on site installation, hosting contracts (ASP), support, update services, additional services and customization, Software as a Service (SaaS) delivers software functionality without the overhead of owning and operating the application.

It is only in the last couple of years that the SaaS model has flourished. According to a listing on Wikipedia, several important changes to the way we work today have made this rapid acceptance possible:

- Almost everybody and every organization has a PC;
- Almost every PC is connected to the Internet;
- Applications are becoming more and more standardized;
- Web systems are becoming reliable enough;
- Online payment is becoming accepted and reliable enough;
- Security on Internet transactions is becoming sufficiently well trusted.

Software as a Service can be characterized as follows. There is no software purchase, licensing, installation or distribution. All SaaS offerings are fully net-native technology. They are no longer based on 'old school' client server applications with HTML front end. In SaaS, the customer can choose from a set of services (function sets), and only pay for the services to which he subscribes to. Thus the customer only gets one periodic bill, that is related to the services he uses. The user can change, add or cancel services any time. Software updating is a continuous process and does not reach the customer as an update. All essential updates are available to the user the next time he logs into his account. SaaS is also characterized by an 'open' environment where the vendor's own technologies fuse with open source and partners. Finally, SaaS services are characterized by minimal customization and minimal preferences. If you like the service, you sign up. If you don't like it, you don't.

We believe that 2007 will signify a breakthrough in the emergence of these kinds of concepts. What we currently see happening is that also large companies including Google and Microsoft are already introducing services based software solutions in their labs or in beta-form. Many smaller companies are building very successful businesses based on the new concepts; for example, 37Signals, Inc. has signed up nearly 500,000 users in less than a years time in Project Management.

In their online book Getting Real they describe the core philosophy of SaaS. The benefit to the user became their number one focus and priority. While the software industry quickly moves towards a serviced-based model, they stated that the reality might be setting in that the market for software will no longer tolerate the so called 'unbalanced cost versus functionality dilemma'. This implies that at 37Signals, within their SaaS implementation, only the most used functions were included in product releases, those used by the majority. For any additional, specialized function they launch another service available for sign up. They no longer package functionality in one huge unit; it is split-up in clear functional pieces and only ordered and digested by the customer when there is a clear hunger. This also implicates that the new SaaS concept does not allow for long product cycles, but for a constant flow of action, extremely short implementation cycles and immediate practical use of breakthroughs and developments.

Essential pieces

We believe it is important enough to call the SaaS movement a new software paradigm. Here are the SaaS fundamentals, inspired by 37Signal's Getting Real, and how we see the library industry benefiting from this.

SaaS is less complicated software, sometimes even 'no software'. The Internet is the basis for making SaaS happen. For software as a service, all the customer needs is an Internet connection and an Internet Browser. No application, no installation, no configuration, no updating. SaaS stands for less of everything that is not essential to the user. It is not that hard to imagine how large parts of today's library software could be split-up into functional pieces. Many of those functional pieces, in particular on the user side, can be offered as a service over the Internet. The software applications are broken up into essential pieces, services that libraries can subscribe to when they need them. What we inevitably see happening is the core library system, the database functionality, the vault and all user-oriented functionality coming apart. It is the latter part that we expect to be dominated by the SaaS model.

Library Vendor Challenges

Everything about SaaS starts, and ends, with the interface. The interface consists of the set of screens used to provide the service. What the user experiences and expects is essential; SaaS intends to build the product from the front to the back. First, the interface needs to be perfected before dealing with the technology behind it. The technology behind it must be hidden completely. Most currents applications are written the other way around. There is a huge piece of technology that we must operate through an interface. The interface then, becomes the last 'part' attached and very little thought is given to it.

What we have described as the 'old' way of building software applications is exactly what happened to the OPAC in its development stage. The search technology that went into the backside was the focus. Only rather than creating a smarter way to search, the OPAC became a complicated, over-engineered monster that few actually mastered well enough to perform really thorough searches. The last part of the OPAC that was given any thought was the interface, which is also why it was/is so user-unfriendly.

SaaS also stands for lowering the cost of change, and therefore, the cost of usage for the user. It uses the web as the podium for constant improving. The user does not need to wait for years to get the next round of improvements. The old idea of having to wait a year or so for the vendor team to get in and install the new update will be fading away sooner than we realize. With the true web-based platform, the software allows for constant product improvement and updating. In fact, the process of getting the improvements may remain completely unnoticed by the user. There will be no more time wasted on downloading application updates and modules, not to mention the horrors involved in uninstalling previous versions. Web-based software, within the SaaS philosophy, can be constantly improved on a minute-by-minute basis.

Change resistance

The library market is by nature slow to change as an industry. This is partially because libraries are typically resistant to change. When innovative practices are introduced there is a slow trickle-down movement. This is why we believe library vendors have been able to sell out-of-date technology to their customers and have gotten away with it for so many years. But this is a finite situation. The times are changing and such attitudes can not continue indefinitely according to the next story. It is a metaphor in which the resistance to change is a clearly painful, from the time of the ancient of the library.

It is the year 336 BCE. Codomannus - a distant relative of the of the royal Achaemenid dynasty - became king of the Persian Empire. He had been put on the throne by the traitor and assassin Bagoas, a former commander-in-chief, who had murdered the kings Artaxerxes III and Arses and most of their families within two years. Codomannus, a distinguished champion in combats, took the regal name Darius III and quickly demonstrated his independence from his murderous 'benefactor' by forcing him to drink poison himself. The throne was now his alone and he was king of the largest empire of the time. Surely, nothing could happen to him now, or Persia?

Codomannus probably chose the name 'Darius' in honour of Darius the Great who had established Persia as the largest territorial empire of the classical period. When Darius I (the Great) died in 485 BCE after thirty-six years of reign, his empire measured 7.5 million square kilometres (about 10 times the size of modern Germany), stretching from present day Turkey in the west to modern Afghanistan and Pakistan in the east, from the Caucasus in the north to parts of the Arabian peninsula, Egypt and Libya in the south. Persia was in control of the Mediterranean Sea, the Red Sea, the Persian Gulf and the Arabian Sea.

The wars, which he fought with a well-organized and equipped army, were not meant for expansion but to gain and maintain strong natural frontiers for the Empire. Size mattered for quite a while and

Darius the Great seemed to prove that a heterogeneous empire was possible. But was it really?

Shortly before his death, Greek war parties began to nibble rebelliously at the borders of his Empire, which resulted in failed Persian punishment expeditions, such as the lost battle of Marathon. The Persian Wars had begun…

Battles with different Greek cities and city-states continued in subsequent decades, but the Persian Empire held on to its size, relative power and wealth. But, not all was well.

> The wars, which he fought with a well-organized and equipped army, were not meant for expansion but to gain and maintain strong natural frontiers for the Empire.

All in all, Darius' followers were not able to shape the Empire into an organic whole and to anticipate or prevent separatist tendencies of provinces, let alone react accordingly. Tensions rose within royal households and between the kings. There was a growing dependence on foreign mercenaries (even Greeks!) and thus a weakened combat strength in the own ranks.

Darius III, although a former king of modern Armenia, had no experience at all in leading an empire, let alone an unstable and weakened empire. In 336 BCE, the first year his reign, the real trouble started.

Phillip II, king of Macedon and hegemonic leader of the Corinthian League sent a force into Asia Minor to avenge the desecration of Athenian temples during the second Persian War and to 'liberate' Greeks living under Persian control. Phillip was assassinated, the campaign was suspended and his inheritor, Alexander, first had to consolidate his control of Macedonia and the rest of Greece.

Alexander, later called the Great, was a pupil of Aristotle and probably the most brilliant strategist of his times. He started to invade Asia Minor in 334 BCE at the head of a combined Greek army of 35,000 and

Risen - Why Libraries Are Here To Stay

almost immediately faced and defeated an equal Persian force – sent by Darius III - at the river Granicus. Persian pride played into his hands. Convinced of their superiority they engaged in a pitched battle (a battle where time and location is set) with Alexander's forces. Alas, the Greeks were better organized, trained, had better, modern equipment and – with Alexander – the better tactics and moral. Although the Persian cavalry outnumbered his, Alexander succeeded in driving a wedge into their formation. The satrap who led the battle was killed and the Persian formations broke and ran for their lives. Western Asia Minor lay open for Alexander.

After this, Darius had to take the Macedonian-Greek threat seriously. But did he really? All we know is that Darius did not reorganize or modernize his vast army. And he still underestimated the Macedonian leader.

Alexander the Great was prepared. He had formed an army of the best specialists he could gather from different parts of Greece and Macedonia. He relied on three important arms that made full use of the then up to date promise. The cavalry, of which the heavy cavalry were his arms of decision: a crack force of the best professional soldiers on horseback with the best horses, heavily armed and protected. Secondly, there was the phalanx, a rectangle of heavy infantry – at that time eight men deep - with spears up to six metres long. The soldiers of the phalanx were disciplined professionals, trained up to a high level. And thirdly, there was the well-trained and swift infantry. Alexander was a master in using these disciplined and agile units tactically and very efficiently. And he could rely on the loyalty of his generals and commanders.

Most of Alexander's successes on the battlefield have been due to separating parts of the enemy lines and fix them into place with the rigid – but agile - phalanx. The heavy cavalry would then attack the flanks of the enemy unit in wedge formation and break it open, wreak havoc and thus leave a wide gap for the infantry to finish the job. This tactics was used with devastating effectiveness, especially in the battles against an enemy, which outnumbered him by far: the battle of Issus and the battle of Gaugamela, the final blow to Darius III and the Persian Empire.

At Issus Alexander faced a Persian army - led by Darius himself – which was almost three times larger. The battle was furious, but Alexander's light troops, helped by the phalanx' succeeded in encircling the Persian cavalry. And then Alexander started the charge with his heavy cavalry straight at Darius himself, easy to spot in his golden chariot. Darius panicked and fled and once the king was seen abandoning the field, the Persians collapsed and Alexander took Darius' wife and family hostage. That was in 333 BCE.

After this victory Alexander decided to concentrate on the control of the coastal areas where most of the cities surrendered but one, Tyre. After a blockade Tyre surrendered as well and Alexander continued to Egypt, where the satrap decided not to stop him. Alexander became Pharaoh and founded the city of Alexandria.

Observations and cures

In the new software paradigm, the old rules no longer apply. Alexander introduced a set of new rules that which blew the existing establishment away. Here is an overview of some of the observations 37Signals made and the set of solutions they proposed.

Observation No. 1: Software is too complex.

There are too many features and there is way too much to learn. Software products have become so complex because of the following two main reasons: The first is that the software company has added and implemented all the features that the competition launched in order to 'keep up' in the market. The second that the software company has implemented all the features their few large, high-end customers (less than 20% of their installed base) have asked for.

Cure: Cut functionality, split up into pieces and make the software as simple as possible.

SaaS identifies product functionality that in essence fills everyone's needs. SaaS modules offer fewer, but more mainstream, features that are used, rather than fill them with features that hardly anyone uses. In most cases, SaaS modules offer less than their competition, however, all essential functionality is in there. The product's functionality is aimed at the critical users' demands; the functionality is no longer aimed at following the competition. All questionable functionality has disappeared. There is one real winner: the user. It is because they will notice that there is an easier and more efficient way to now do what they always wanted to do.

Observation No. 2: Interfaces are too complex and completely not user-friendly.

Most product interfaces are built on the old software paradigm of complexity. Huge collections of functions are hidden under huge numbers of pull down menus. Customers need training to learn the proprietary logic of the functions. There is no standardization in it. Apparently most applications started with a program- and technology-first mentality. The interface seen as the result of the technological and programming choices made in the process.

Cure: Make the interface the best part of the product.

In the new software paradigm the interface is designed before the programming is started. The interface becomes the product, since what the users will see is what the library vendor is selling. If everything begins with the interface, the function follows form. In web design for a user-interface it is far more important to focus on the user. The programming of core technology is by far the most expensive part of the product. Design and user interface in contrast are cheaper and much easier to manipulate. A healthy focus on design of the user interface keeps the vendor close to their customer needs and constantly close to the latest industry advancements. Programming first boxes them in, creates huge cost and keeps the end-user at a distance from the final product.

Observation No. 3: Most products lack excitement.

On any new feature or product introduction the user has to react with excitement. "This is great", "finally we have it" or "wow, this is what we really need". The last thing we want is users to react with yawning or by furrowing their brows. Real excitement is what every product enhancement is all about, but what has been missing for a decade in the library industry.

Cure: Never stop making exhilarating improvements.

It is the library vendor's challenge to never ever stop the creative process on any product function. We believe there is always room for real improvement. The fulfilment of any specification is treated as an interactive process to excite the user. When any function is introduced, the library vendors should follow it, ask the customers for feedback, question it honestly and keep improving it. The cure is to stay beyond the users' expectations. Take little, useful steps in digging deeper and understanding why. Any development or improvement, no matter how small it may be, will reflect on the whole chain of products in a positive way.

Observation No. 4: Most products are sluggish.

Most products, their development cycle and interactivity with the user, can be best described as sluggish. They have a sluggish feel. There is no lightweight agile feeling; there is a large amount of inertia, lethargy in both product operation and maintenance.

Cure: Think that products and services to be built for change.

Any product that responds quickly and interacts directly is received positively. There is a lot to gain in innovation that is directed at generating product responsiveness, speed and agility. We believe that there is a lot to gain in critically evaluating and developing products out of this angle, and the pursuit of true speed and agility.

Observation No. 5: Most software companies lack responsiveness.

Most large companies are characterized by time-consuming processes and meetings. Product specification cycles, planning features and arguing details with the goal of making everyone happy, alpha testing, beta testing, pre-launch and final launch are commonplace. The general perception is that there must be absolute consensus on what is right for the customer with the highest demands before launch. Maybe the difficulty lies in the fact that larger software companies are organized in a wide range of functional departments. Every product enhancement needs to go through all the stages.

Cure: Cut out all the unnecessary parts.

In the new software paradigm products and product functionality are associated with being lightweight and agile. Minimized multi-disciplinary teams are linked to products and services on a one on one basis; each product has its own multi-disciplinary team. Teams are built out of a maximum of 5 to 7 people, any larger team proves inefficient. Meetings are reduced to only the most necessary. Within a team, software development and support communicate and work together, sharing the responsibility of customer-care. Checking the competition is eliminated and transformed into an entire team that is focused on the specific part of the market and the user, obtaining feedback and using it for future innovations. The development team is not busy copying the competition but instead, is thorough in ensuring customer satisfaction. The determining factor is user satisfaction. Creating and maintaining documentation can be reduced significantly because the simplicity of the product interface doesn't require complex training. Because there is no licensing and transfer of rights anymore there is a minimized legal department. There are no binding customer contracts; the customer can check out from the services as easily as he could check in.

It is in the ILS vendor's hands

ILS vendor companies operating in the new paradigm are small, or have fewer, smaller departments. Instead of long product (update) cycles, there are constant incremental improvements that reach the user. All development efforts are focused towards the user, the user interface and the web user interface in particular. The competition is checked, not followed. Development and support work closely together. There are no rigid definitions to departments. Rather than being confronted with a junior support employee, any one of a number of experts would help the client when there was a need.

In marketing and sales, the product website plays the essential role, both in promotion and in sales. In essence, it is the software 'storefront'. Expenses on trade shows and brochures are kept at a bare-minimum. The simplicity of the product and the focus on the user interface allows for much less documentation. All documentation is built into the online product. And since the product is not sold to the customer – instead the product functionality is offered as a service through the web - there is no need for complex licensing terms and conditions. Since the new software paradigm does not ask the customer to sign binding contracts for 3 or 5 years, there is no need for an extensive legal review of the sales agreement, no negotiation and no added cost.

All development efforts are focused towards the user, the user interface and the web user interface in particular. The competition is checked, not followed.

The library industry is notorious for the old fashioned cumbersome software models of yesterday. The new software paradigm is the perfect fit for this industry because for the most part, libraries do not have the time, or the money to waste on outdated methods. Libraries mostly rely on public funding, and that makes efficiency an even higher priority.

With the new software paradigm the library can choose the necessary services it needs to provide the best functions for its patrons. This will vary by community, by type of library, by size, and by collection. The options available will be the best suited for each library, without bothersome 'customization'. The software would then become available instantly and offered through the web-based application, rather than enormous files being set up on a dedicated server, sometimes taking months and hundreds of man-hours. The library would have an instant online catalog, open, constantly updated and upgraded with no effort, or even awareness from the library personnel.

We envision that only a part of the current ILS industry will be able to follow and make the transition. It is very tempting to continue harvesting profits from the current installed base and the on-going long term agreements. We still believe that those vendors who will not be able to change their business models and embrace the services model will slowly disappear. We see new parties entering the marketplace, offering essential, but limited, spot-on functionality. This is what happened with the Project Management market and 37Signals. We also envision large modern IT players from outside entering the library market, offering integrated generic functionality with 'just good enough' functionality for well defined subsets of the market.

As long as the library customer is placed at the top of the chain, there will always be room for the best players in the library vendor market. The key here is that every company should focus 100% on that at which it excels, and that the customers have the critical functions available to them at all times.

Conclusion

The library has many opportunities and possibilities where even the slightest change can make a huge difference. What was our 'doom scenario' at the beginning of this book; the acceptance of average and the mediocre, was meant as a warning of what could be.

We are only as limited as we make ourselves out to be.

There is a very different story that could happen in the world of the public library and the library vendors.

In 2007 and 2008, both sides of the table could focus on accessibility. Searching could become better, faster and easier. The aggregation of more and more sources could become further reaching from more investment in digitizing collections, as well as new agreements that could be made between library clients and the data-licensing agents and information providers.

Once things are set in motion, and the focus on search and accessibility, sources aggregation and quality-stamp recognition is coming together, the value of the library can be truly reflected in the library's web identity. In the years 2009 and 2010 the roles of the library vendors may be extremely important. Where they are competing today through the 'me-too' modus of business, they could begin to work with the technology that exists outside of the library realm. The best ILS vendors could be doing very diverse and truly innovative schemes by 2010. While there will be a 'catch-up' period from now until that year, the vendors will manage because there does not have to be a total replacement of the way they work now, at least not immediately. Instead they could openly integrate new solutions into their current models in long-term plans, keeping customers happy who demand specific attention and customization right alongside with gaining new business through focus on the masses.

What would it take to get people into the library? Once the library's focus shifts towards accessibility, it is prudent that the public know about it. The web identity of the public libraries would have to be as clear as any search engine: you are here to search for information; we are here to provide the best information available, instantly. Marketing the library in a whole new way is a part of this plan.

Turning libraries into modern institutions with all of the right design, functions, tools and personnel to promote free access to information is only half of the job at hand. The focus would also have to encompass changing the world's presumptions and opinions of libraries for it all to be truly effective. By 2012, the library could be seen as the information guide, where the very best collection of information and knowledge is made freely available to everyone.

We strongly believe everyone involved within the library realm can take the responsibility and steps necessary to retain this invaluable tool for the future. As stated before, we believe the public library is already the guardian of information, the realm and protectorate of the information democracy. It is powered by dedicated people committed to serving the greater public good. The library is filled with validated facts, diverse opinions, a multitude of qualified resources, a wide array of potential useful technologies and the flexibility and intelligence to cope with our need to have information instantly and conveniently.

It is probably that the Internet only represents a small portion of the information and knowledge mankind has gathered since his beginning.

Conclusion

The conclusion drawn here is that if we use the Internet as our sole source when looking for real sets of trustworthy relevant information, we leave everything to chance.

Search and web accessibility are key. Focus on the role of being the guide to information will lead to spending lots of energy and resources aggregating and opening up local and specialized resources – all in a single search. People can and will think of the library as their primary source of information; they will learn how to find and access the content of the collections in and outside the library, from any location, at any time. The users will demand something better because they will suddenly realize they were becoming average and nearly stopped questioning altogether. Library vendors will follow with innovative web-based solutions that answer the demands of the library users and information professionals.

The library vendors will need to see what is really happening outside the library realm. They will have to acknowledge that software is too complex. They will have to scale down the product complexity and design and offer products that the customers really want. Some of the vendors will have to take a good look at their own means of operating. The companies themselves will have to scale back, and reassert their main missions to be able to focus on the customers.

The interfaces the library vendors are offering will also have to change for anything functional to matter. The interfaces will have to be easy to use, easy on the eyes, and designed in ways that help and not hinder the product usability. These interfaces will have to become good enough that users only identify with them, and not all that is going on in the background, and this goes for the library professional user as much as the library patrons. The complexity of most library system interfaces will have to disappear and be replaced with genuinely well-designed interfaces that anyone will want to use. It is in the library vendors' hands.

The fact that society must be able to swallow is that the library is not the dusty old place of 'yore'. It is not the quiet, musty room our teachers took us when we were children and teens to do research, using a card catalog that was too delicate to touch from the library staff, and too complicated for us to use. The revolution in media and the growth in the information and knowledge management industry has never been more apparent.

Which ever side you see it from, that technology has pushed the access to information to a higher demand, or that our demand for information has pushed technology to new levels, the library is not what it used to be. The technology that did almost take power away from the library in the past decade is now being used to give it back. And the library professional is actually a computing and technological expert that is ready and jumping at the opportunity to help patrons find what they are looking for.

The issues we have discussed in this book are not meant to be rules or guidelines; they are simply the main issues we see in the library industry from both the vendor and the library's positions. If the library is to continue to play a vital role in society and the world and not be overcome by technology that at best offers generic and average-grade information, then it is up to the library realm as a whole to step up to the plate and take responsibility. Part of that will be updating the image of the library both physically and online, and part of that will be the library vendors offering something new, different and truly innovative to the market.

By 2012 the library can become a true powerhouse of information and the first place we think of when we have a question, any level, any form, on any topic.

Risen - Why Libraries Are Here To Stay

Inspirations

Below is a list of resources that helped inspire us to write this book. All of our inspirations come from either people or organizations that have very specific web identities.

Find more about...

..."gardening" in a library catalog:

www.queenslibrary.org

..."dogs" in a library catalog:

www.nypl.org

..."Johannes Vermeer" in a collection of library sources:

www.oba.nl

...Apple's latest iPod:

www.apple.com

...Nokia's latest mobile:

www.nokia.com

...booking a flight with The Royal Dutch Airlines:

www.klm.nl

...library catalog search "as a Service":

www.aquabrowseronline.com

Furthermore, *Risen* is inspired by:

The Software as a Service movement:

www.wikipedia.org/wiki/Software_as_a_Service

A SaaS company that revolutionized project management:

www.37signals.com

A worthwhile strategy for (public & academic) library management:

www.blueoceanstrategy.com

A worthwhile strategy for ILS vendor management:

www.blueoceanstrategy.com

The myths and legends we learned from storyteller Peter Fruhmann, The Storybag:

www.addition.nl

Kathy Sierra's writings on creating passionate users:

headrush.typepad.com

Find out more about the authors and the company they work for:

www.medialab.nl

Find more about a few of the OPAC critics and commentators whose blogs we read:

All the great writers and staff at The Library Journal

www.libraryjournal.com

Karen Schneider

freerangelibrarian.com

David Lee King

www.davidleeking.com

Inspirations

Sarah Houghton-Jan

`librarianinblack.net`

Jenny Levine

`www.theshiftedlibrarian.com`

Edward Vielmetti

`vielmetti.typepad.com/superpatron`

Risen - Why Libraries Are Here To Stay

Notes

Risen - Why Libraries Are Here To Stay

Notes

Risen - Why Libraries Are Here To Stay

Notes

Risen - Why Libraries Are Here To Stay

Notes

Risen - Why Libraries Are Here To Stay

Notes

Risen - Why Libraries Are Here To Stay